THE
WORLD
ON A
PLATE

THE
WORLD
ON A
PLATE

A Tour Through the
History of America's
Ethnic Cuisines

JOEL DENKER

Westview
PRESS

A Member of the Perseus Books Group

Copyright © 2003 by Joel Denker

Westview Press books are available at special discounts for bulk purchases in the United States by corporations, institutions, and other organizations. For more information, please contact the Special Markets Department at the Perseus Books Group, 11 Cambridge Center, Cambridge MA 02142, or call (617) 252–5298 or (800) 255–1514 or email j.mccrary@perseusbooks.com.

Published in the United States of America by Westview Press, 5500 Central Avenue, Boulder, Colorado 80301–2877 and in the United Kingdom by Westview Press, 12 Hid's Copse Road, Cumnor Hill, Oxford OX2 9JJ.

Find us on the World Wide Web at www.westviewpress.com

A Cataloging-in-Publication data record for this book is available from the Library of Congress.
ISBN 0–8133–4003–9
The paper used in this publication meets the requirements of the American National Standard for Permanence of Paper for Printed Library Materials Z39.48–1984.

10   9   8   7   6   5   4   3   2   1

TO PEGGY
for her joyous spirit and for
her faith in me and my dreams

CONTENTS

ACKNOWLEDGMENTS

This book could not have been written without the cooperation of food makers, their relatives, or staff who took time from their busy lives to talk with me. They listened patiently as I posed sometimes mystifying questions and pressed them for obscure details. Many thanks to Frank Uddo; Michael Uddo; John Taormina; Charles Sahadi; the late Joe Shuad; Robert Colombosian; George and Nawal Rababy; Marios Christodoulides; George Vallianos; Harold Kullman; Stanley Leavy; the late Sanford Claster; Aaron Gilman; Elliott Gabay; Mohammed Afzal and his brother, Tariq; Syed ("Jay") Siraj Din; Louis Giatras; Conrad Colon; Cresencia Torres; Rafael Toro; Luis Salcedo; and Karen Sperling.

I much appreciated the help of Doreen Moses, who lent me a video copy of her film *One on Every Corner*, a portrait of New York City's Greek-owned coffee shops. Doreen was enthusiastic about my work and shared her knowledge of the Greek food business with me.

Rabbi Jeffrey Marx was kind enough to provide me his chronological history of the Breakstones' business.

Margaret D'Arrigo Martin, Vice President of D'Arrigo Brothers, gave me a very useful commemorative pamphlet on the history of the company.

Libraries, archives, institutes, and other organizations helped me probe for missing pieces of this puzzle: the American Italian Federation of the Southeast, in New Orleans (Joseph Maselli, chairman of the advisory board, sent me lots of material); National Italian American Foundation; the Hammonton, New Jersey, Historical Society; the

Faris and Yamna Naff Family Arab-American Collection, Archives Center, National Museum of American History; Andover, Massachusetts, Historical Society; Lawrence, Massachusetts, Historical Society; Chinese Historical Society of America; University of Minnesota Immigration History Research Center; Center for Migration Studies; and Goya Foods Collection, Archives Center, National Museum of American History. Toni Jeske, Assistant Archivist of the University of Texas–San Antonio Archives, and Kendra Trachta, Library Director of the Institute of Texan Cultures, were most generous.

The Inter-Library Loan service of the Gelman Library at George Washington University Library promptly and helpfully located hard-to-find volumes for me.

My colleagues in the George Washington University History Department, Edward Berkowitz, Bill Becker, and Leo Ribuffo, encouraged me while I pursued the project, listened to my discoveries, and seemed genuinely interested in an area outside their own specialties.

I am grateful to the community of writers, scholars, and other food experts who took time to answer my questions, offer leads, send materials, and share insights: Vincenza Scarpaci, Rose Scherini, Harvey Levenstein, Donna Gabaccia, Alan Kraut, Felice Bonadio, Anthony Margavio, Joe Logsdon, Thomas Karnes, Alixa Naff, Mary Ann DiNapoli, Philip Kayal, Robert Mirak, Timothy Lloyd, Charles Moskos, Peter Dickson, Andrew Kopan, Peter Makrios, Richard Gutman, Lawrence Lovell-Troy, Tom Bailey, Jenna Joselit, Bruce Kraig, Joan Nathan, the late Richard Shepard, Charles Wong, Madhulika Khandelwal, Sidney Mintz, Andrew F. Smith, James Trager.

Pat McDonough, who is too modest to acknowledge his profound contribution to the book, was immensely helpful. Regina Wise helped me meet what often seemed like an impossible deadline.

Burr Lowrey and Maxine Schiffman, partners in a book group, listened to a writer's tribulations and cheered me on.

Fellow members of an essay group responded to my writing when its focus was beginning to crystallize and urged me to spin out my ideas. Thanks to Marguerite Beck-Rex, Krystyna Edmondson, Mary

Weideman, Burr Lowrey, Nancy Arnesen, Larry Lesser, and Peter Slavin.

Much of this book was written at Jolt 'N' Bolt, a coffeehouse in my neighborhood. I am grateful to Farooq Munir, the proprietor, for offering me a sanctuary, an ideal home away from home. He was unusually patient with the idiosyncrasies of an author maddeningly searching for his muse. His staff was invariably gracious and the high-octane lattes were marvelous.

A portion of Chapter 7 was drawn from articles that originally appeared in Washington, D.C.'s *The InTowner* newspaper. I very much appreciate the paper's permission to use this material. Peter Wolff, the publisher of the paper, has provided me a perch to survey ethnic food and culture for more than ten years. It was a rare opportunity to test out ideas and writing approaches. Peter freed me to carry out what must have seemed to him very unusual forays into the world of food.

I had wonderful companions on excursions to ethnic restaurants: Don and Nina Britcliffe, Fred and Barbara Cooper, Ed and Marian Shor, Debbie Luxenberg, Steve Johnson, Joe and Tammy Belden, Mary Gill. The members of the "Ethnic Chowder Dining Society"—Jim and Barbara LaRock, Linda Holloway and Ed Nusbaum, Jerome and Maxine Schiffman, and Carolyn Wyatt and Mike Moore—were superb dining adventurers.

Carol Mann ably represented me in this venture. Jill Rothenberg, my editor, helped bring a sometimes unconventional manuscript to fruition. Barbara Greer was a most efficient project editor, while Ida May B. Norton handled the copy editing with precision.

My wife, Peggy, to whom the book is dedicated, helped me every step of the way—with everything from the smallest details to turns of phrase. She lent her keen technical proficiency and ear for style to the project. When I was most discouraged, she stayed buoyant and encouraged me to keep going.

Invitation to a Journey

BEFORE IT BROKE INTO THE mass market, yogurt was a "secret" whose appeal was limited to the Middle Eastern community, Charles Sahadi, the Lebanese food magnate, remembers. A struggling Armenian family, who made yogurt in a backyard workshop on their Massachusetts farm during the Depression, was an early manufacturer of the product. The Colombosians, who started out peddling their homeland staple in horse-drawn wagons, in time began selling the item to supermarkets. They called it Colombo, because so many people couldn't pronounce their name.

The journey of ethnic food from the alien and unusual to the familiar and commonplace is a recurrent one in America. Kebabs, spring rolls, and samosas today are following the same path that yogurt blazed many decades ago. Jaded consumers, we take our polyglot foods for granted. We also rarely know, or at least forget, the origins of everyday products. How many of us realize that broccoli, of southern Italian lineage, was once regarded as a strange, unappetizing vegetable? Or that its popularity was the result of an astute marketing campaign recounted in this book?

My book uncovers the hidden saga of immigrant food makers, past and present, and the foods they have introduced. Written for a general audience, its object is not to instruct or analyze. This folk history first and foremost aims to tell the colorful story of the contributions that unsung ethnic groups have made to our culture.

1

The book, a long time in germination, springs from my enthusiasms and curiosities. For as long as I can remember, I have avidly sought out restaurants that offered unusual fare—a Cuban-Chinese eatery in New York City, a Turkish grill house in Boston, a Filipino restaurant in San Francisco's "Little Manila." These excursions combined the pleasures of earthy food and the thrill of discovering immigrant outposts.

Traveling and teaching abroad intensified my interest in diverse cultures. I wandered the streets of Bradford, an English mill town transformed by Pakistani immigration, and explored Southall, a London suburb known as "Little Punjab" because of its large Sikh community. I savored spicy grilled beef and chapati and sipped passion-fruit juice at an Arabic café in the old quarter of Dar es Salaam, a city on the Indian Ocean that is the capital of the East African country of Tanzania.

I infused my writing with similar passions. As a columnist for *The InTowner*, a Washington, D.C., newspaper, I sought out ethnic restaurants—Trinidadian, Persian, Indonesian—whose variety belied Washington's image as a white-bread city. I also ventured farther afield, roaming and writing about Newark's Portuguese Ironbound neighborhood and describing the ethnic byways of Montreal.

My teaching and intellectual interests gradually merged with my delight in food. I took my gusto into the classroom. A course in cultural anthropology at a Boston community college became an investigation into the foreignness of America's customs and cultures. My companions in this search were ideal. They were young adults from the city's ethnic neighborhoods. In other teaching, I have benefited from my encounter with blue-collar New Yorkers, Southern black high school students, and West African graduate students.

I have also been a student and teacher of American history. A book on the story of our ethnic food was a marvelous way to bring together my interest in America's immigrant past with my engagement in food and culture.

☆ ☆

A central theme of *The World on a Plate* is that food and folkways are inseparable. It looks back into the lore of kebabs and chili and examines the way that foods as different as smoked fish and choy (Chinese leafy vegetables) anchored the lives of immigrants in a strange land. Traditional foods also metamorphosed into new forms to please American consumers. Yogurt was sweetened, and complex Indian dishes were watered down. Old-country products are now sold in new ways—herring is packaged in jars, Latin spices are mixed and packaged, and cheesecake is displayed in the frozen foods aisle.

Food is also part of a larger human story, the adventures of bold immigrants struggling to boost their fortunes. Food not only linked them to their past but also became a source of present livelihood and future advancement. Aspiring countermen, food peddlers, grocers, and restaurant operators feverishly pursued the American dream. As they scrambled up the ladder, they left an indelible imprint on our food. Their achievements encouraged later arrivals to pursue a similar path.

The leading figures in this book are the folk heroes of the ethnic food trade. The sweep of the business is embodied in tales of farmers as well as manufacturers, of importers and retailers. Interviews with many of the central characters, their descendants, or associates put flesh on their stories.

You will meet Giuseppe Uddo, the one-time Sicilian peddler of cheeses, olive oil, and tomato paste, who founded Progresso Foods. You will accompany Nathan Handwerker, the young Polish Jewish immigrant who popularized the spicy, all-beef frank at Nathan's Famous, his Coney Island eatery.

I hope this book will transport you to the varied regions and communities that were wellsprings of ethnic food. Chinese food is chronicled on the Rocky Mountain frontier, chili in San Antonio, Greek-American confectionery in Chicago, and "hot Texas wieners" in Paterson, New Jersey. You will discover food entrepreneurs in unexpected settings: Giuseppe Uddo launched his business in New Orleans. Two Pakistani businessmen, Mohammed Afzal and his brother,

Tariq, who run the Ravi Kabob restaurant, operate in a lower-middle-class neighborhood in Arlington, Virginia.

The World on a Plate does not pretend to be a complete or exhaustive account of this vast subject. Nor does it offer a seamless history or a chronological narrative of the development of ethnic food. I have chosen instead to offer tantalizing tastes of the food experiences of seven ethnic groups, past and present.

My chapters are designed to take readers on a historical tour. They often encompass different stories, locales, and characters. The chapter on Italians, for example, travels from California to New Orleans and on to New York and New Jersey as it follows ventures in agriculture, the produce business, tropical-fruit importing, and food manufacturing. A loose thread connects the different stories, which could equally well stand alone.

Similarly, a chapter with a huge canvas like the one on Latin food resists facile unity. Instead, I have developed two long essays, relating two radically different but equally representative dimensions of the story, one on the evolution of Southwestern chili, the other on the merchandising of Caribbean and Latin American food by Goya Foods, a New Jersey–based company.

The boundaries between chapters are likewise loose. William Gebhardt, a German immigrant in New Braunfels, Texas, who introduced chili powder, appears in the chapter on Latin food. Jeno Paulucci, born to an Italian immigrant mining family in Aurora, Minnesota, is featured in the chapter on Chinese food. Paulucci founded Chun King, which would become the country's largest seller of canned and frozen Chinese food. Immigrants in America do not confine themselves to tidy compartments, and neither, as I hope to show, does their food.

Finally, I welcome stories and responses from my readers. You can reach me at denker@starpower.net.

CHAPTER 1

·······················

That's Amore:
Italian Food in America

Have you ever seen an Italian family attack a washtub full of salad?
Or a caldron of broccoli? Or a bushel of string beans? Or a peck of
tomatoes flanked by cucumbers and peppers? Or have you seen them,
just by way of priming themselves for the main course, sit down to a
kettle of endive cooked in broth? . . . Somewhere in every Italian there
lurks a caterpillar.

Angelo Pellegrini
(*Americans by Choice,* New York: Macmillan, 1956)

The Produce Kings

FIG TREES AND GRAPEVINES grew in the backyards of many an Italian immigrant. Italians clung tenaciously to their eating habits, persisting even in the face of the suspicious attitude of locals. They had a special zest for produce and were adept at growing and preparing it. These passions were reflected in their strong presence in the fruit and vegetable business as farmers, merchants, and manufacturers.

California was an early seedbed of Italian agricultural enterprise. California, the mythic "Queen of the Pacific" to the immigrants, had America's largest Italian population (2,805) in 1860. The long coastline and temperate climate of northern California, the favored region, reminded the new arrivals of the Mediterranean. Unlike the waves of

5

southern Italians who swept into America during the late nineteenth and early twentieth centuries, California's frontiersmen were primarily northerners from Liguria and Tuscany.

Miners, who panned for gold in the Sierras between 1848 and 1851, broke the ground for later settlers. Italians gravitated to San Francisco's Latin Quarter, an international district near Telegraph Hill, where they joined French, Basque, and other European immigrants. The Italians, who lived in fishing shacks and cottages along the narrow streets of the Hill, gradually moved during the 1860s closer to North Beach, which became the center of their community. Both settlements were close to the harbor, where their boats were docked, and in walking distance from the waterfront, where a large number worked as fishermen.

In North Beach, the Italians tried to re-create the lively commercial quarters of their homeland, *"un piccolo canta patria,"* a small corner of the mother country. Groceries, *trattorias* (restaurants), cafés, bakeries, and other businesses dotted the streets. In time, North Beach would become the headquarters for the Bank of Italy, import houses, merchant firms, and larger ethnic businesses headed by northern Italians.

On the outskirts of San Francisco, Italian farmers, fellow ethnics of the North Beach settlers, were digging up the sand dunes and hilly soil and planting lettuce, spinach, bell peppers, strawberries, and other crops. The *"giardinieri,"* as they called themselves, followed the path of the horse-car lines with brooms and dustpans gathering the precious manure for their plots. As early as the 1860s, pioneering truck farmers, some of them former gold miners, were cultivating *basilico* to sprinkle on minestrone and to make pesto sauce. These northern Italians, most from the Genoa region, also grew rosemary, thyme, oregano, marjoram, and fennel. They sold the herbs first to French and Italian settlers in the city's Latin Quarter. Gradually, native San Franciscans incorporated the fragrances in their cooking.

The agriculturalists also popularized bell peppers, zucchini, fava beans, and other produce. Bay Area catalogs in the 1890s advertised artichoke seeds. In Oakland, the James Hutchinson nursery in 1874 began promoting eggplant to home gardeners. In 1910, Italian farmers in Half Moon Bay, south of San Francisco along the peninsula, shipped the first artichokes to arrive in East Coast markets.

Ethnic farmers introduced locals to the plum tomato, which had previously been an Italian export item. In Merced, in central California, Camillo Pregno, an Italian immigrant, showed farmers how to grow tomato vines on stakes. The Italian method produced ten times as many tomatoes as the older practice of open planting.

The farmers developed their own distribution systems. In 1874, San Francisco *giardinieri* set up a produce outlet, the Colombo market, in the center of the city. From the outer peninsula, they hauled their vegetables by horse and wagon to the colorful site, around which hotels and boarding houses sprang up. "The rich, earthy smell of bruised and crushed vegetables was everywhere," a local reporter wrote. "Bearded, swarthy, brawny Italians in red flannel Garibaldi shirts darted about with their dark hands stained red by the blood of beets."

The *giardinieri* put their products in the hands of northern Italian merchants. Genoese from Liguria handled the transactions in the market and often advanced the farmers funds until they were paid for their goods. Tuscan peddlers hawked the vegetables throughout San Francisco.

Market gardening spawned new food businesses. Marco Fontana, the immigrant founder of the California canning industry, moved to San Francisco after a stint of mining. The Ligurian son of a marble cutter found a job working as a clerk for Gallo and Company, a merchant house in the Colombo market run by a countryman.

The experience taught him valuable lessons. He noticed the vast amount of waste in the market. Fontana took bruised fruits and vegetables home, where he experimented with canning them on the stove of his back porch. The more he tinkered, the more convinced he became that canning could become a profitable avenue. Produce that might otherwise go to waste could be preserved and canned. Canning could expand the market for California farmers to the East, where customers were looking for a substitute for fresh produce in the winter months.

Fontana created his own canning business and then, in 1899, formed a syndicate of other canners, the California Fruit Canners Association, which controlled the state market. The entrepreneur built the world's largest cannery in North Beach, near Fisherman's Wharf, which processed asparagus, peaches, pears, and other products under the brand name Del Monte. He tapped his ethnic network to hire a predominantly Italian workforce of 1,000 women. From this building block, a larger corporation, Del Monte, was fashioned in 1916 to serve the national market.

☆ ☆

In 1928 bunches of broccoli from California with distinctive pink labels that said "Andy Boy" began arriving in Boston grocery stores. The broccoli had been packed in ice and transported in Western Pacific railcars. Two young Sicilians, Andrew and Stephen D'Arrigo, were trying to transform an ethnic vegetable into a brand-name product.

The teenagers, whose father was a lemon farmer in Messina, arrived in Boston, where their cousins ran a produce business, in the early 1900s. After working in shoe factories and at other jobs, Stephen and Andrew joined the U.S. Army in 1917, just as the country was entering the war. After the war, the brothers became partners with their cousins in a business that sold grapes to immigrants for making wine. In 1923 they broke away and started their own firm.

The D'Arrigos stuck with the grape business. Stephen moved to California to oversee the shipments, and Andrew stayed in Boston to handle their marketing. As a result of living in San Jose, a town with a large Italian community, Stephen turned his attention from grapes to other produce. Farmers in the area were growing prickly pears, fennel, and broccoli, plants he knew from his native Sicily.

The young Sicilian was especially intrigued by broccoli, a vegetable with a long Italian tradition. Adored by the Romans, the ancient

Mediterranean plant got its name from *brocco,* the word for sprout or shoot. Broccoli probably originated with rabe, a mustard resembling turnip greens that grew wild in the hills. When rabe was mated with cauliflower, the offspring was broccoli.

Encouraged by the success local farmers had with broccoli, Stephen experimented by growing his own with seed first sent him by his father. The trial was successful, and he bought a twenty-eight-acre ranch in San Jose. Stephen and his farm workers harvested broccoli, tied bunches with raffia twine, and hauled it to a packing shed in San Jose, where it was packed for rail shipment to the East Coast.

The D'Arrigos sensed a business opportunity. Except for a small crop in Brooklyn, little broccoli was being grown for the region's large market of southern Italians, who had the greatest appetite for the vegetable. With a little coaxing, the brothers hoped that northern Italians, who knew less about broccoli, would also buy it. By capitalizing on California's longer growing season, the D'Arrigos were convinced that they could deliver a large supply of broccoli during the winter months to shoppers in Northeastern cities.

In 1924 the D'Arrigos tested the market. Stephen shipped a few crates of broccoli to Andrew in Boston, where Italian customers snapped them up. They decided to increase shipments with their own brand name on the boxes. The gimmick didn't work: Some grocers replaced the D'Arrigo broccoli with a cheaper, mediocre vegetable. To prevent counterfeit sales, the brothers devised a pink band-type label to be wrapped around each individual bunch. Pictured on it was the cherubic face of "Andy Boy," Stephen's two-year-old son, Andrew, who loved traipsing in the broccoli fields with his father. On the wrapper were recipes and cooking instructions.

Branding their vegetable had several objectives. The label was designed to set their broccoli off from the competition. If "Andy Boy" became synonymous with quality, superior farming, handling, grading, and shipping, customers would pay premium prices for it.

The D'Arrigos backed up their brand with radio advertising, the first use of the medium to promote a vegetable. In 1928 the company bought spots on a Boston Italian-language radio program. In Boston and later on New York and Philadelphia stations, nutritionists explained the virtues of Andy Boy to housewives. D'Arrigo farmers, they said, handled the tender product with exquisite care in order to conserve its rich store of vitamins and minerals.

In the stores, D'Arrigo's sales representatives trained clerks in the technique of caring for a vegetable that could easily wilt or spoil. They handed out leaflets, set up store displays, and put on demonstrations of how to prepare Andy Boy.

Andy Boy was also advertised in newspapers, on billboards, and on subway posters. Expecting that the American consumer would now be receptive, the D'Arrigos expanded to English-language radio. Between 1943 and 1946, Andy Boy sponsored the *D'Arrigo Serenaders*, a musical program on WBZ, a Boston station. It built an audience by promoting premiums like a $1.00 steamer for cooking asparagus and broccoli.

The promotions paid dividends. The company's sales jumped from twelve carloads of broccoli in 1924 to more than one thousand in 1945. To extend its growing season, D'Arrigo shifted its production from San Jose to the Salinas Valley, which had cooler temperatures.

The company took other previously unfamiliar items and popularized them. Using seed from Nice, France, D'Arrigo marketed the country's first Pascal celery. One afternoon at our local Safeway I spotted a new product sporting a pink Andy Boy label. It was a bunch of broccoli rabe, the wild green that had long been an Italian secret. A recipe for Cheese Pie, a mixture of rabe, ricotta, and Parmesan cheese, was printed on the back of the label.

☆ ☆

Joseph Di Giorgio, the titan of California's fruit industry, created a national corporation that controlled produce from the field to the point of sale. Both in scope and in capital, it far surpassed the D'Arrigos' enterprise.

Di Giorgio, who became the country's largest grower of grapes, plums, and pears, grew up in Cefalu, forty miles east of the Sicilian capital of Palermo. Peppino, as young Joseph was called, was raised on his father's lemon farm. He was sent to the seminary but had little taste for the priesthood. He dropped out of school and went back to the farm. His father, who headed a cooperative of lemon growers, decided to send the fourteen-year-old to New York City with a shipment of fruit. Until the early twentieth century, Sicilian farmers supplied the Northeast with most of its lemons. In New York and other cities, their compatriots dominated the import business and ran most of the fruit stands.

Di Giorgio arrived in 1889 and began working for a *paesan*, who was his father's lemon broker. For eight dollars a week, he worked in the Washington Street produce market. The budding trader left five years later for Baltimore, which had a large colony of Cefalutanos engaged in the fruit business.

Di Giorgio began peddling fruit and, with a $700 loan from a countryman, soon opened a shop selling lemons. When the citrus business slowed during the winter months, he imported bananas. Di Giorgio began with two bunch lots and expanded to larger shipments. He soon chartered steamships to bring fruit in from Cuba, Jamaica, and Honduras, three to five thousand bunches at a time.

Di Giorgio outgrew wholesaling and seized on a new merchandising technique, the auction house. In 1904 he launched the Baltimore Fruit Exchange, the first in a series of firms that the tycoon would own or take controlling interest in. At the auction house, the buyer received his fruit twenty-four hours after the sale was made. The arrangement was more efficient than the older, more cumbersome system of individual wholesalers. "This was the perfect method of distribution of perishable produce," Robert Di Giorgio, Joseph's nephew, pointed out. "It could be moved quickly."

Since he needed a steady stream of fruit to feed his auction machine, Di Giorgio borrowed money from the railroads and acquired the Earl Fruit Company, a fruit-packing house in Sacramento, California, in 1910. Owned by Armour, Earl refilled railcars that had carried meat to California with fruit and sent them back East. To keep his farmer suppliers afloat, the new owner lent them money to plant their crops, buy tools, and purchase supplies. Frustrated with carrying overextended growers, Di Giorgio resolved to eliminate the middleman and grow his own fruit. He went scouting for land in the San Joaquin Valley, the southern half of California's vast interior central valley.

On one visit near the present-day town of Arvin, Di Giorgio observed the earth after it had been soaked by a heavy rain and dreamed of the harvests he could reap. The long growing season and the dry climate would enable figs, grapes, and apricots to flourish. "The idea of going into the Di Giorgio farms area was for earliness of maturity," Robert Di Giorgio recalled. "Because the early bird got the hottest prices. And it was the warmest place to start."

In 1919 the magnate bought 1,000 acres, a harsh tract of sand, cactus, and sagebrush. Crews cleared the arid land, dug wells, and pumped groundwater. "We went in there with twenty-horse mule teams, because there weren't tractors big enough to do that work at that time," Robert Di Giorgio recounted. "They used to pull the plows and do the land leveling and prepare that land. It was absolute desert. There was nothing there. No water there, and there was no Arvin."

Never paying more than $90 an acre, Di Giorgio accumulated more land for fruit ranching. By the time of his death in 1951, he had assembled 10,000 acres. Rows of grapes—Malaga, Cornichon, Emperor, Thompson Seedless—ripened on the vine, and trees bursting with plums, peaches, and apricots grew in the once-unforgiving Arvin soil. Gazing at one of his properties, the titan was exultant. "All this I create myself. Before I drill the wells, all was desert." To ensure a continuous supply of fruit, he expanded north to capture pears, a cold-weather crop, and farther south to garner grapes that ripened earlier.

Combining peasant savvy and corporate know-how, the Sicilian merchant created a national fruit corporation that brought the abundant produce of the West to the kitchen tables of the East. Di Giorgio controlled all sides of the business. Fruit traveled from the fields to his packing sheds, where they were packed in crates manufactured in his Klamath Falls, Oregon, box factory. Di Giorgio's freight cars carried the crates—1,000 loads a year in the 1930s—to company auction houses in New York, Baltimore, Chicago, and other cities.

After the bidding was over, the merchandise was whisked from loading dock to buyer. "When the auctions would start selling early in the morning, they would be through by eleven o'clock, and by two o'clock that afternoon, every single box of fruit, two hundred and fifty carloads of fruit would be off the dock and delivered to the buyer . . . and then that next morning . . . that fruit would be at the Waldorf Astoria," Robert Di Giorgio said. "It would be at the A & P. It would be at the pushcart on Second Avenue. It would be in the restaurant, at the club."

Di Giorgio, whose father had also owned a small vineyard, planted grapes on a massive scale. In the early years, he reserved a large share of his biggest crop for the Italian market. He shipped hundreds of railcars eastward filled with grapes that were bought by home brewers. Although this ardent "fresh grower" was not initially interested in wine making, Di Giorgio stumbled into the business. Because his grapes were frequently prey to frost, disease, and fickle markets, he resolved to convert the unused fruit to wine. This was a "method of taking a perishable crop and giving it a shelf life," Robert Di Giorgio pointed out.

In 1931, Di Giorgio, who had recently suffered through a bad harvest in which many of his grapes dried on the vine, paid a chance visit to the Italian Swiss Colony vineyard in Sonoma, California, ten miles north of San Francisco. A Genoese immigrant, Andrea Sbarboro, had bought this land in 1881 when it was a 1,500-acre sheep farm. Planning to transform it into a cooperative vineyard, he hired unemployed northern Italians and Italian Swiss, who were accomplished grape pickers. Because of falling crop prices, the colony decided to produce wine. Sbarboro supported the vineyard with a loan from the Italian American Bank, the bank he had founded in San Francisco.

Ten miles north of San Francisco, Swiss Colony, which had the world's largest wine tank, was hurting. It was using only a tiny portion of its production facilities. Di Giorgio proposed a deal—he would provide Swiss Colony the next two years' grape harvest in exchange for a share of the company. In return, Swiss Colony would crush the grapes and store them to sell at the end of Prohibition. The parties agreed, and soon gondola cars were hauling grapes from the Di Giorgio farm in the central valley to the Asti vineyard.

When Prohibition was repealed, Sbarboro was poised to conquer the wine market. He bought back Di Giorgio's wine for $250,000 and "very dramatically blanketed the United States with their product," Robert Di Giorgio said. Tipo chianti, the Swiss Colony brand, was wrapped in a distinctive raffia cask. For the first time, Italian wine makers were challenging the dominant German and French producers of pricier white wines. Once derided as "dago red," the stuff of immigrant basements, red wine was becoming respectable.

Rather than having to depend on other vintners, Di Giorgio began producing his own wine. He bought a winery near Delano in 1933 and built his own facility on the Arvin ranch. The direction made good business sense, Robert Di Giorgio observed. "You had to salvage your own because otherwise you were at the mercy of the processor. . . . Winemaking . . . was a method of getting the last possible gross dollar out of the harvest of the grapes. Because if you didn't use those grapes, you couldn't make money growing fresh grapes."

Passage from Palermo: The Italian Food Business in New Orleans

Before the Civil War, ships were traveling between Palermo, Sicily, and New Orleans with cargoes of lemons, oranges, and other citrus fruit. Trains left New Orleans bringing fruit to the Midwest and West and returned with grain and other products to be exported to Italy. The Crescent City was becoming the capital of the fruit trade between the Mediterranean and America.

Citrus, which was then scarce in the United States, grew prolifically in Sicily. The island's Arabic conquerors had been passionate cultivators of oranges and lemons. They adored the fruit for its beauty and fragrance. In Spain, North Africa, and their other possessions, the rulers decorated palaces, mosques, and villas with sparkling orange groves. Visiting a villa near Palermo, a Sicilian poet was awestruck by a "blazing fire" of oranges "amongst the emerald boughs." Sicilians embraced the bitter, blood and double blood oranges, tangerines, citrons, and the other varieties that their tropical climate blessed. During Christmas, the islanders displayed oranges or tangerines in their nativity decorations.

The fruit trade carried many of the early Mediterranean immigrants to Louisiana, which in 1850 had America's largest Italian population. Ships sailing from Palermo carried both passengers and citrus fruit. Many of the Sicilians getting off the SS *Utopia* in New Orleans in 1888 toted small containers of lemons. They had worked in their homeland as fruit farmers or fruit peddlers.

Merchants with ties to old-country farmers and shippers set up businesses in New Orleans to import and distribute fruit. They, in turn, recruited laborers from Sicily experienced in unloading produce. Others peddled carts of fruit through the city.

Unlike San Francisco, a preserve of the northern Italians, New Orleans would become a bastion of the Sicilians. Its semitropical climate, Mediterranean tempo, and Catholic traditions reminded them of home. They "recreated their world," historian Joseph Logsdon argued, in this American Nice.

Locals both praised and damned the immigrants. The *Daily Picayune* of New Orleans editorialized in 1890: "We of New Orleans owe to the Italians a vastly larger obligation than New York owns to. It is mainly through Italian enterprise and capital that the importation of foreign fruits at this port has been developed from a mere peddling

business conducted in a few sailing schooners, to the dignity and pro-
portions of a great commercial interest."

Joseph Macheca, who owned the city's largest shipping company and
held the honorary title of Consul of Bolivia, symbolized the aggrandiz-
ing Italians natives resented. Macheca, the stepson of the firm's founder,
traded in citrus fruit from Sicily and also opened up a market in bananas
and other tropical fruit from Central America. The New Orleans business establishment bristled at the power this upstart exercised over the
docks and the French Market, for which he was a major supplier.

When David Hennessy, the New Orleans police chief, was killed in
October 1890, Macheca was arrested with seven other Sicilians and
accused of organizing a conspiracy to carry out the assassination.
Macheca, it was alleged, was pursuing a vendetta against Hennessy for
favoring the Provenzanos over the Mantrangas, two stevedoring clans
who were fighting for control of the docks. A crowd jeered, "Who
killa de Chief?" at the van carrying the prisoners to jail.

A jury acquitted the eight arrested men on March 13, 1891. Furious
at the verdict, a mob led by some of the city's leading citizens marched
on the jail the next day and killed eleven Sicilians. Three months later,
an unrepentant mayor, Joseph Shakespeare, castigated New Orleans's
Italian immigrants: "They monopolize the fruit, oyster and fish trades
and are nearly all peddlers, tinkers or cobblers. . . . They are filthy in
their persons and homes and our epidemics nearly always break out in
their quarter. They are without courage, honor, truth, pride, religion or
any quality that goes to make the good citizen."

☆ ☆

Hostility did not slow the fruit business. Joseph Vaccaro, who would
become the tycoon of tropical fruit, found his first job in 1867 working in the rice fields on the Magnolia Plantation downriver from New
Orleans. The native of Contessa Entellina in Sicily, who had just a
third-grade education, peddled *napoli* (apples), shoelaces, and other
items. Vaccaro gave up hawking and got a job harvesting sugarcane. In

a few years, he had saved enough money to buy a small piece of land to truck farm.

Early every morning he hauled his vegetable wagon to the French Market in New Orleans, usually arriving by dawn. His grandson, Joseph D'Antoni, describes the fierce competitor: "As a rule, his was the only wagon there at that hour. Communications in those days were very poor, and the owners of produce stands had no way of knowing what other wagons might appear and at what prices their produce would be offered. So they bought out my grandfather at top prices. On his way back to his farm with his wagon empty and his money in his pocket, he would meet his competitors coming in, with loaded wagons."

In typical Sicilian fashion, Vaccaro joined up with another immigrant family, the D'Antonis, who owned a general store near Baton Rouge. Joseph Vaccaro and his two brothers, recently arrived from Sicily, sold their partners' produce. After a flood in 1897 destroyed the shop, the Vaccaros and D'Antonis started an orange venture. They would buy out the crop from plantations in the levee country downriver and ship them up in luggers, small boats, to New Orleans. The oranges were delivered to Joseph Vaccaro, who sold them from a stall in the French Market.

In January 1899, Salvador D'Antoni married Joseph's daughter, Mary. Three weeks after the wedding, the deep South's worst winter devastated the orange crop and crippled their budding business, forcing its owners to change course. As Joseph D'Antoni tells it, "It was then that Joseph Vaccaro said to his son-in-law, my father: 'If we are to achieve our ambitions in life, there is not much left for us here. I understand that there are coconuts and bananas in Honduras.'"

They bought an aging two-masted schooner, the *Santo Oteri*, named for one of the city's Sicilian fruit merchants, which sailed for Honduras on December 7, 1899, with Salvador D'Antoni at the wheel. On its early voyages, the merchants loaded up with coconuts and smaller cargoes of oranges, the fruit they knew best. The *Oteri* carried only a few banana parcels. Since bananas required sturdier and swifter boats, the Vaccaros soon began sending out steamships to transport the more lucrative product. Often hauling more than 200,000 stems a trip, the company rapidly captured the Honduras banana business.

The Vaccaro brothers ran the New Orleans shipping operation while the D'Antonis worked out of Honduras. The company expanded, acquiring banana, citrus, and coconut plantations and building its own railroad line from the port to the fruit groves. To prevent their bananas from ripening too rapidly, the company built a mechanized storage plant along the railroad line. In addition, Joseph Vaccaro, who became the "ice king" of New Orleans, bought up all the city's ice plants. The brothers named their produce colossus the Standard Fruit and Steamship Company. Standard's achievements helped make New Orleans the world's largest fruit importer in the early twentieth century.

The shippers had to fight their way to victory. They battled Gulf storms and heat waves and fended off rival importers. The city's xenophobic climate almost crippled the business. When a yellow-fever outbreak in Honduras in 1905 spread to the Gulf Coast, New Orleanians blamed Italians and the fruit merchants for spreading the infection to the city. The Vaccaros suffered for four months while the port barred banana shipments in and out of New Orleans.

On October 5, 1925, more than 600 of Louisiana's notables, including the state's senators and governor, gathered at the Roosevelt Hotel in New Orleans to salute the Standard clan's entrepreneurship. St. Clair Adams, the president of the Louisiana Bar Association, lauded the families for lifting New Orleans "out of the mud" and transforming it into a "beehive for useful activity."

☆ ☆

The Italian colony in New Orleans, once dominated by fruit merchants and *prominenti*, notables and men of means, was reshaped by tides of ordinary Sicilians who descended on the city in the latter part of the nineteenth century. Between 1880 and 1910, fifty thousand Sicilians passed through the port of New Orleans. The infusion spurred the growth and diversification of the food industry.

The city's business leaders talked openly of their desire to coax more immigrants from the Mediterranean. These European colonists "would bring with them and introduce the modes of producing their various fruits and wines," leaders at a business convention in 1867 fervently hoped. "The waste fields, now deserted, would, under their patient labor, become fruitful with the grape, the olive, the fig, the orange, the lemon."

Sugar planters, who were looking for a new supply of pliant hands to replace a recalcitrant black workforce, used their state's ties with the island to recruit Sicilians. Some of the new arrivals left New Orleans for the sugar parishes along the Mississippi that encircled the city.

The *zuccarata*, the annual sugar harvest, ran from October to December. The Sicilian peasants cut cane with their machetes and at night toiled in the sugar mills grinding, cooking, boiling, and refining the product. They were paid sixty cents a day. Although the owners preferred the immigrants to the blacks, they still considered them peons, "black dagos."

Some "birds of passage" went back to Italy after the harvest. Others stayed on in the state, typically quitting their jobs after two harvests, the time it usually took to acquire a stake. "By that time they have laid by a little money and are ready to start a fruit shop or a grocery store at some cross-roads town," one business magazine noted at the time. "Those who do not establish themselves thus strap packs and peddle bluejeans, overalls and red handkerchiefs to the Negroes."

Truck farming was another popular pursuit. Adept at extracting vegetables from stubborn soil and small plots, the immigrants grew artichokes, chicory, zucchini, eggplant, and bell peppers. Sicilians planted cucuzza, a long, pale green squash eaten during the summer, and cardoon, a thistle related to the artichoke.

Farmers were a crucial link in the food empire the immigrants were building in New Orleans. They sold their fruits and vegetables to kin or countrymen, who peddled the produce in the neighborhoods or sold it from stalls in the French Market. Italian merchants were taking over the market, which began to resemble a Palermo bazaar. "A riot of smells," Richard Gambino wrote, it was fragrant with "musty vegetables, pungent fruits, sweet flowers."

The immigrants also opened bakeries, restaurants, and ice cream parlors and carved out a niche in the grocery business: Italians ran almost half of New Orleans's food stores in 1920. Groceries served as a combination store and lunch room. The *mufaletta*, the quintessential New Orleans sandwich, was a specialty of the Sicilian grocery. Conceived in the early 1900s at the Progress Grocery, a shop near the French Market, the round loaf bulged with layers of ham, salami, and provolone. It was dressed with a Sicilian olive salad, a mixture of olives and pickled carrots, celery, cauliflower, and other vegetables.

The newcomers transplanted a culture, sociologist Anthony Margavio observed, that "revolved around food." Marrying southern Italian cooking with Creole cuisine, they developed a hybrid style. The immigrants introduced stuffed eggplant and artichoke dishes and incorporated local seafood—shrimps, crabs, and oysters—into their repertoire. They infused New Orleans food with garlic and tomato sauce.

☆ ☆

The burgeoning Italian community clamored for tomato paste, anchovies, cheeses, and other products that only their homeland could supply. Sicilian importers like Giuseppe Uddo, the founder of Progresso Foods, responded to this craving. The eldest of six children, Giuseppe grew up in Salemi, a small Sicilian village twenty-five miles from the Mediterranean. After the third grade, he quit school to help support his family. The nine-year-old drove a horse-drawn cart selling olives and cheeses in Salemi and nearby towns. Giuseppe was a *venditor*, a traditional Sicilian vocation.

On one of his trips, the peddler met Giuseppe Taormina, a successful food merchant, who had many relatives in New Orleans. Taormina took to the young salesman and introduced him to his daughter,

Eleanora. The two married and decided to try their luck in New Orleans. Giuseppe and Eleanora, both then twenty-four, sailed from Palermo and landed at the Canal Street docks in 1907.

Since the food trade was "all he knew," his son Frank said, Giuseppe went to work for his brother-in-law, Francesco Taormina, who had an import business. He lost the job when Francesco closed down to return home to fight in the army. Eleanora's cousins, also food merchants, hired Giuseppe to work in their warehouse.

The Uddos lived in a crowded tenement in the French Quarter, which was dubbed *Piccola Palermo* (Little Palermo). They shared a toilet with the other dwellers. Laundry hung in the outside courtyard.

Giuseppe was stranded on Christmas Eve of 1909 when his employers went bankrupt. He now had two young children to support and wondered what he would tell his wife. On his way home through the French Quarter, he met a Mr. Cusimano, who owned a macaroni factory in the district. Cusimano asked the disconsolate Sicilian what was worrying him. After hearing Uddo's tale of woe, he offered him goods to start his own business and promised him credit to buy more.

Giuseppe was ready to strike out on his own. He had a supply of olives, cheeses, and tomato paste but no way of transporting them to sell. He went back to Eleanora's cousins and implored them: "If you're going to go bankrupt, give me your horse." They agreed and Giuseppe borrowed the money to buy Sal. A godsend, "the horse knew where to go," Frank said. Since his father adamantly refused to learn English, he depended on the horse to take him on the sales routes to Italian customers. According to Frank, this was the beginning of Progresso: "The horse started the business."

Giuseppe left home about 3 A.M. to travel to Kenner, Harahan, and other Italian truck-farming communities outside New Orleans. "The roads were terrible and the mosquitoes were so big, you could put saddles on them," his son, Salvadore, told the *New Orleans Times-Picayune*. After three days on the road, the peddler returned home and prepared his wares for another trip. He and his wife spiffed up and relabeled the cans of tomatoes they had gotten from Cusimano.

As business grew, Uddo expanded his venture. He replaced Sal and bought trucks. He purchased a small warehouse in the French Quarter on Decatur Street, installing his family upstairs to live and running his peddling operation below. He also opened a grocery on the ground floor and placed his brother, Gaetano, recently arrived from Sicily, in charge.

Just before World War I, his father, Frank remembered, decided to "gamble everything." Giuseppe took out a loan and bought three thousand cases of tomato paste. When an embargo closed Italian ports, Uddo's sales boomed, and he used his profits to bring the rest of his family to New Orleans. His parents, Salvadore and Rose, and his sisters, Tomasa and Francesca, joined him. The patriarch made all his family members stockholders. Giuseppe "did not believe in paying salaries," Frank said.

After the war, Uddo bought a factory in Riverdale, California, owned by the Vaccaros, the New Orleans fruit magnates, which manufactured tomato paste. He sent his brother Gaetano out to run it. The plant was the first in the United States to make the product, which had previously been available only from Italy. The war had taught Uddo that it was too dangerous for his company to rely exclusively on imports.

Giuseppe was always dreaming up new enterprises. He started New Orleans's first movie theater, built a cigar-rolling factory, and opened a ship chandler's business in Galveston, Mississippi. But he was "never a good follow-up man," Frank discovered. Once he began making candles in the back of his warehouse, but they all melted in the city's torrid heat.

The California cannery was turning out more tomato products than the company could sell in Louisiana. Uddo wanted to tap new markets, especially in the rapidly growing Italian enclaves in the Northeast. "There are more people in New York than there are in Rome," he told Frank.

Giuseppe joined forces with the Taorminas, the members of another Sicilian trading clan, who had begun a struggling import business in New York City. Frank G. and Vincent Taormina, distant cousins of Eleanora Uddo, and their cousins, Frank R. and Eugene, were floundering when Giuseppe rescued them. Giuseppe advanced the Taormina "boys," as he liked to call them, vital capital and brought his family to New York in 1930 to help out the firm. Three years later, Frank G. Taormina married Giuseppe's daughter, Rose Marie. As Frank Uddo tells it, this alliance "cemented things" in the Uddo-Taormina company, the newly merged enterprise.

Francesco Taormina, Eleanora's brother, sent olives, *pomidori pelati* (peeled Italian plum tomatoes), and other staples from Sicily to their Brooklyn headquarters. The California tomato cannery sent carloads to New York for distribution. Olive oil was shipped from Tunisia, where Giuseppe's cousin owned a factory.

Sicilian imports poured into Brooklyn. The business sold sardines, anchovies, and *incanestrato*, a cheese molded in a wicker basket (*canestro*), to ethnic groceries. It roasted peppers and marketed salted chickpeas (*ceci*), which Italians snacked on during feast days and other celebrations. *Caponata* was a signature item. The Sicilian appetizer, a traditional summer dish, combined eggplant, tomatoes, onions, and celery in a sweet-and-sour blend made piquant with capers, olives, and anchovies.

The company prospered. It developed a clientele among both retailers and wholesalers. The major Italian middlemen who worked the Northeastern market bought large orders of Uddo-Taormina tomatoes. "We were playing both ends of the stick," Frank Uddo, who was now working with the company, said.

World War II boosted sales. "During the war you could pack anything and sell it," Frank said. The company had to increase domestic production because "they couldn't import any product," John Taormina, Vincent's son, recalled. In 1942 they bought an old factory in Vineland, New Jersey.

The southern Jersey plant was in the heartland of Italian farmers. Settlers from southern Italy got their start as strawberry and raspberry pickers or as railroad or brick workers in the late nineteenth century and soon saved enough to buy their own land. The rugged pinelands soil was soon producing a bounty of melons, pumpkins, tomatoes, eggplants, and other fruits and vegetables. The farmers grew grapes and made wine. Emily Meade, the sociologist and daughter of Margaret Mead, visited nearby Hammonton in 1907 and marveled at the Italian innovations: "Italians have popularized the sweet pepper and introduced . . . a peculiarly shaped squash, okra, Italian greens, and various kinds of mint."

The Vineland plant, Frank Uddo said, had the "largest smokestack on the East Coast." Workers canned and bottled roasted red peppers, sweet fried peppers, pepper salad, hot cherry peppers, tomato sauce, crushed tomatoes, tomato puree, and other products. Flo Alvino, who was hired to do the payroll for farmer suppliers, fondly remembers her early, exciting years with the company: "Farmers' trucks were lined up on the boulevard. You could smell tomatoes all over Vineland." Inside the plant, "women were cutting peppers by the handful." Others "lined up on both sides of the conveyor belt looking for blemishes."

Since farm vegetables were seasonal, the company started looking for a year-round product. Soups were the answer. From family recipes, it produced hearty, fibrous minestrone, thick with vegetables, beans, and pasta, and lentil soup, made from a bean beloved by the Romans. They developed a version of *pasta e fagioli* (pasta fazool), a mixture of broken-up pasta and beans in a tomato and salt-pork sauce that Italian immigrants subsisted on. Flo Alvino called it "mac and bean." After the war, the Vineland plant was turning out the country's earliest ready-to-serve soups: This was the beginning of Progresso soups. "The sideline became our major line," John Taormina pointed out.

From soups, they moved to beans, another peasant mainstay. A novelty for many Americans, they were a meal to the Italians. Fava beans, another favorite of the ancient Romans, became a filling dish after being mashed, mixed with greens, and dressed with olive oil. The Vineland business marketed cannellini, pinto, chickpeas, and black beans and changed the American diet.

Shoppers were now less fearful of ethnic products. Returning GIs "had been exposed to Italian food," said John Taormina. More and more consumers in postwar America, including many from immigrant backgrounds, were now doing their buying at the supermarket. By marketing primarily to small grocery stores, however, Progresso was losing business. The company, plant manager Vincent Taormina argued to his colleagues, had to crack the chains. Other officials countered that this would mean losing older customers who could not compete with lower prices in the supermarkets. "You'd lose the foothold in the Italian deli," John Taormina summed up their views.

Vincent Taormina carried the day. Progresso "made the leap into the supermarkets" in the late forties, John Taormina said. In the New York area, Acme was their first customer, and other chains followed. Frank Taormina went on the road, calling on stores in the South. He made a pitch to the Winn-Dixie chain. "I talked them into opening an Italian section in all their stores." This became the Progresso formula—displaying its array of products in one space—and the example encouraged other immigrant enterprises. "This was the whole start of the ethnic foods that you see today," John Taormina observed.

A new brand name began appearing on the company's products. The Progresso label was based on a pastel painting Giuseppe Uddo had bought for $150 many years before at the Progress Grocery in the French Market. Drawn by one of the brothers who owned the shop, it portrayed "progress" through the rise of new forms of transportation. The symbol of improvement appealed to new and older Americans alike. Having the same name as the most popular Italian-American newspaper, *Il Progresso*, also made it attractive to ethnics.

Progresso advertised on radio and television. It hired an advertising agency that sent a soundtruck through Italian villages during World War II to record "letters" from family members to their American relatives. The *Grande Famille*, the radio program Progresso sponsored, broadcast these messages on Northeastern radio stations in the late forties. The company also sponsored Bishop Fulton Sheen's television sermons during the fifties.

Once unusual, the products Progresso unveiled in the supermarkets have become commonplace. Its canned tuna in olive oil was a Sicilian favorite that gained a wider following. An early twentieth-century Sicilian entrepreneur, Ignacio Florio, who was the first to manufacture the canned fish, made it an everyday item on the island. *Tonno*, the island's favorite fish, enriched pasta, rice, and bean dishes.

Pine nuts, minced clams, capers, artichokes, and other specialty products also grew into household staples. Bread crumbs, both plain and Italian-style seasoned with fennel, garlic, and other spices, became one of the company's largest sellers. Olive oil and bread crumbs, which "were big in the Italian community in New Orleans," Frank Uddo said, gained national popularity.

The Uddo and Taormina clans fought over the control of Progresso after the death of Giuseppe Uddo in 1957. The founding father, a rock of stability, had kept the two sides at peace. When animosities threatened the survival of the business, the owners agreed to sell the firm to Imperial Tobacco, a Canadian corporation, in 1969. Pillsbury, which owns the company today, acquired it in 1995.

Michael Uddo, Frank's son, is carrying on the Progresso tradition at the G and E Courtyard restaurant in New Orleans, located right around the corner from Giuseppe's old headquarters. He has vivid memories of growing up in the import business. "Something was always coming in," he recalled. He filled containers with olive oil and packed Greek olives, sometimes gorging on them until he was sick.

"Everything was done through the family," Michael said. "We were required to be at meetings because we had stock." The clan gathered for lunches of braised veal tongue, roast chicken with garlic and rosemary, and other dishes prepared by his grandmother, Eleanora. Michael models his restaurant on Sicilian traditions. "It's based on the same principles—rustic Italian food."

···························

CHAPTER 2

From the Fertile Crescent:
Yogurt Peddlers and Falafel Kings

Tins of olive oil with gaudy labels in French and Arabic, water pipes, their stems tasseled in scarlet and bright lemon . . . heaps of cream and purple eggplant and russet pomegranates . . . streamers and foamy piles of fine-meshed lace . . . Turkish vases, their enamel an intricate kaleidoscope.

Writer **Will Irwin**, who visited New York City's
"Little Syria" neighborhood in 1926, describing
the store windows' sensuous delights

"The Mother of All Colonies"

NEWCOMERS, MOST OF THEM Christians from the Mount Lebanon region of the Turkish colony of Syria, began streaming into New York City, their favorite port of entry, at the turn of the century. Twenty thousand immigrants had arrived by 1920. "They began coming in small groups in the garb of mendicants," Edward Corsi, a former immigration commissioner, observed. "They wore red fezzes, short baggy blue trousers, to the calves of the legs and ill-fitting shoes." Although they were Christians, who identified themselves as Syrians, they were commonly branded as Turks, a heathen race. After World War II and their homeland's independence, the immigrants would begin calling themselves Lebanese.

27

Typically young, single men from the countryside, small landowners, traders, and skilled workers, the immigrants were fleeing an ailing economy and the oppressive Turkish army. Recruited by steamship agents and enticed by stories of riches to be reaped, the Syrians abandoned their villages. "All of my village of Ayn Arab rushed to America," one pioneer put it. "It was a gold rush." The men trekked by foot and donkey to Haifa, Jaffa, and other Middle Eastern ports for the trip to Marseilles, where they embarked on the long voyage to "Amrika."

They founded their largest colony at the tip of Manhattan, a short walk from where their boats tied in. Washington Street, a seven-block strip that social worker Lucius Miller called a "dumping ground for new arrivals," was the enclave's center. Dutch burghers had once occupied the district's ancient brownstones. The French, the Irish, and the Italians had camped out there. Nearby, sedate Wall Street squeezed against its boisterous neighbor, whose noisy streets now reverberated with the shouts of vendors hawking gold bracelets, Turkish delight, anise, and other spices.

The newcomers "huddled in crowded apartments," merchant Joe Shuad said, and crammed into hotels and boarding houses with the other bachelors. To escape the suffocating loneliness, they congregated in coffeehouses. In the early 1920s, writer Konrad Bercovici observed

> swarthy men drawing the cool smoke from the aromatic titun that burns slowly in the brass container over the large jar filled with rose-scented water through which the smoke passes before it is drawn by the smoker. Small coffee-shells, into which the mud-thick coffee is being continually poured, are being served all around by the large, majestic dark-brown owner of the khava, whose bare feet are encased in pointed, heelless slippers, babouches dragged flippity, flippity, flop as he walks around.

Purveyors of Arabic foods catered to the settlers. Nuah Abaid, a one-time Syrian rug merchant, opened a confectionery shop on Washington Street in 1907. He wove strings of walnuts dipped in grape syrup and prepared apricot paste flavored with almonds. Abaid lured shoppers with violet syrup, rose petal jam, and orange blossom water. Customers stopped to sip a tamarind drink, a tart refreshment made from the sticky pulp in the pods of the "Indian date," the translation of its Arabic name. They feasted on pistachio- or walnut-filled pastries, enriched with butter made from goat's milk.

Habib Shuad's Washington Street shop sold nuts and seeds to the avid Arab snackers. This one-time West Hoboken, New Jersey, silkmill worker made a makeshift roaster from an oil drum. He cranked it by hand over a bonfire, roasting pistachios, hazel nuts, salted chickpeas, pumpkin seeds, and squash seeds.

Syrian merchant Abraham Sahadi ran an "Oriental" grocery, as Middle Eastern food stores were then called, near the nut shop. The store, which Sahadi opened in 1895, was redolent of cinnamon, cumin, thyme, sumac, and other spices. He carried briny olives, chickpeas, fava beans, lentils, and other staples.

He sold bags of bulgur, the nutty cereal that is one of the oldest processed foods. The cracked wheat was essential for tabbouleh, the minty, parsley-laden summer salad. It was also basic to kibbe, the national dish of Syria and Lebanon. Kibbe ("ball-shaped" in Arabic) is the seasoned paste made from pounding ground lamb and bulgur. Dexterous housewives mold the paste into a myriad of shapes—balls, torpedoes, cakes—for dishes that are variously served raw, baked, fried, or grilled.

Sahadi imported sesame seeds to make his most important product line. His company roasted the seeds and ground them to create tahini (from the Arabic "to grind"), the creamy, oily paste that flavors Middle Eastern dips. Mixed with garlic and lemon juice, it perks up hummus, the chickpea spread, and infuses *baba ghanouj*, the smoky eggplant puree.

Sahadi used tahini to make bars of halvah, the crumbly sweet that the Turks popularized throughout their empire. The firm also manufactured sesame crunch candy, apricot delight, pistachio delight, and other confections.

☆ ☆

Syrian peddlers were roaming over North Dakota in 1888.
Louise Houghton,
Literary Digest, May 3, 1919

Washington Street was just the beginning of the journey for many of
the immigrants, especially the young men who were aspiring peddlers.
Peddling was a trade that suited a people who despised working for
someone else. As easily started as dropped, it appealed to the itinerant
Christians. The restless Levantines were happiest when they were
outdoors "smelling air," notes the writer Abraham Rihbani. Peddling
demanded little cash and limited English—a few phrases like "Buy
sumthin', ma'am."

Seeking patrons, the transients attached themselves to wholesalers,
who stored the myriad goods of the trade in their living rooms and
basements: "pins by the hundred gross rest against shoe-blacking by
the case, and scapularies and rosaries, beads and prayer books are almost hidden from view by boxes of cheap cologne and ornamental
shellwork." Their suppliers, merchant Joe Shuad said, "staked them to
a bundle of goods" and sent them off to the hinterland.

After two days on Washington Street, their sponsors took one
group of immigrants to the train station with their destination, Fort
Wayne, Indiana, pinned to their lapels. Other peddlers climbed
aboard trains headed for Oklahoma City, Terre Haute, Vicksburg,
Jacksonville, and other trading outposts. In the spring, many returned
to Manhattan to pick up another consignment.

Wandering the country roads and town blocks, the peddlers carried
a basic grab bag of goods. From their packs they pulled out work
clothes for men and school wear for children. They dangled linens,
doilies, and bedspreads before housewives. Hawkers tempted customers with crucifixes, rosaries, and other gifts from the "Holy Land,"
which were often made in New York. Dipping into their notions
cases, they pulled out thread, ribbons, and lace.

Syrian enterprise paid off. Peddlers hauled in an average of a thousand dollars annually in the decade before World War I, while at the same time sending money home. By the 1920s, the inveterate wanderers were settling down in pockets scattered around the country. They called for family members to join them and gradually abandoned dreams of returning home.

The growing Arabic settlements craved their familiar foods, and merchant Abraham Sahadi decided to tap the market. From his Washington Street headquarters, he shipped his far-flung customers bulgur, apricot paste, beans, and other staples. Sahadi's salesmen went on the road beating the drums for his wares.

Wade Sahadi was one of those peddlers. The eighteen-year-old, who went to work for his uncle in 1919, took the train to Chicago and other cities, often traveling with salesmen from rival companies. Staying overnight at the homes of faithful customers, he took orders from families as well as from the host of stores that were beginning to serve the Middle Eastern immigrants.

Some of the shops were general stores; others specialized in the ethnic foods needed for daily meals, family celebrations, and holiday gatherings. The commercially shrewd Armenians established cluttered shops piled with foods from the homeland, like the one in Chelsea, Massachusetts, Richard Hagopian describes in his novel *Faraway the Spring*:

Manoog's store had all the stinks and smells of a third-rate foreign bazaar. Everything in it looked exotic, strange, and on the verge of putrefaction. There was merchandise strewn everywhere. Long, rigid baloneys and sausage hung from the hooks in the ceiling; barrels of nuts, flour, cracked wheat, and squash seeds lined the walls. Tubs of olives and swimming Greek cheese had been shoved under tables on which rested tins of Armenian pastry, herbs, and all sorts of canned stuff.

Abraham Sahadi's company was expanding. Building on his commercial network, he added a mail-order business to a firm that had become a combination importer, retailer, wholesaler, and manufacturer. Through his firm, America's Arabic settlements remained inextricably tied to Washington Street, "the mother of all colonies."

Wade Sahadi, who, his son Charlie recalled, was more "progressive" than his uncle, itched to strike out on his own. In 1941 he broke away to start his own business. Wade, who had become a partner in the firm, was paid his shares in olives, wheat, and rice. He opened Sahadi Importing Company, not far from his uncle's shop on Washington Street.

☆ ☆

Just across the East River from Manhattan, a small Arab oasis flourishes on Atlantic Avenue. . . . No date palms grow in this part of Brooklyn, no rose gardens perfume the evening air, and the only caravan ever spotted on the horizon is the line of traffic on the Brooklyn–Queens Expressway.

But never mind. Inside the Lebanese stores that form a block–long bazaar on both sides of the avenue, you will find huge mounds of sticky dates from the palm trees of Iraq, coils and coils of Turkish Delight redolent of attar of roses.

Zelda Stern,
The Complete Guide to Ethnic New York (1980)

The immigrants of Washington Street began leaving their dingy and cramped tenements for the greater elbow room of Brooklyn. The South Ferry neighborhood, a nickel ferry ride across the East River from lower Manhattan, was a natural destination. Atlantic Avenue, once Brooklyn's main street, became the commercial hub of the new "Little Syria."

Arabic bakeries were the earliest of the immigrant food businesses on Atlantic Avenue. At the Near East, the oldest of the shops, bakers rolled out their flat bread by hand and baked it in brick ovens. The immigrants called it *khubz*. Outsiders referred to it as "Syrian bread," but never as pita, the name used by Greek gyro merchants.

Wade Sahadi, one of Washington Street's last businessmen, moved his shop in 1947 to the more promising Atlantic Avenue district. In addition to basic cooking ingredients, he sold water pipes, clay water jugs, backgammon sets, Turkish tea glasses, and other exotic items. The store even offered customers frankincense and myrrh.

In the beginning, Sahadi's customers were primarily ethnics. To shoppers unfamiliar with Middle Eastern food, the store appeared mysterious, alien. Charlie, who helped his father, remembers two ladies who walked down the aisles looking quizzically at the walnuts and cashews, the cans of okra and fava beans. One turned to the other and said, "Who would buy in a place like this?"

Habib Shuad also took his nut shop from Washington Street to Atlantic Avenue. He expanded into dried fruit, an Arab passion. His "fruit leather," sheets of dried raisins, grapes, and apricots, became a popular item. The business expanded, manufacturing pistachio brittle, Turkish delight, and other sweets. Shuad began roasting nuts in his own factory.

Ethnic food was not yet in vogue in the 1950s and 1960s. On the Atlantic Avenue frontier, Middle Eastern restaurants were introducing customers to their exotic fare. The Son of Sheik, which had once operated on Washington Street, featured stuffed eggplant, grape leaves, shish kebab, and other Lebanese specialties.

Some Atlantic Avenue restaurants capitalized on their appeal as purveyors of forbidden pleasures. Mama Semrany, who ran the Eastern Star Restaurant, plied adventure seekers with bottled arrack, a potent liqueur made by a local Lebanese moonshiner. She lost her drawing card after federal agents raided her restaurant. The Star and other restaurants regularly staged *haflis*, boisterous wedding parties spiced up with belly dancing, to pull in customers.

Atlantic Avenue was becoming a magnet for Middle Easterners throughout the metropolitan area. On weekends, ethnics from Westchester, Long Island, and New Jersey came seeking foods unavailable in their communities. In one such excursion, the Haddads, a Lebanese clan from Jersey City, descended on Malkos, an Atlantic Avenue grocery. A *New York Magazine* writer describes the scene:

The Haddads from Jersey City explode inward, crashing through the door, filling the corners of the 12 by 20 food store, sampling nuts, pinching dried apricots, opening and tasting jars of candy.

Papa Haddad, mustachioed, proudly flashing his gold teeth, Mama, small and subdued, daughters, daughters-in-law, grandsons and grand-daughters, nieces and nephews, pocketing here, tasting there, surrounding an inlaid table—touching, wondering, debating in Arabic.

Atlantic Avenue was also blossoming into a capital of Arabic culture. Albert Rashid, who, as a young boy, left Syria with a brother fleeing the draft, opened a record and film store next door to Sahadi's grocery. Rashid had started out peddling Arabic movies imported from Cairo to Syrian communities in Cleveland, Toledo, Houston, and other cities. The Rashid Sales Company, which became the nation's largest distributor of Middle Eastern films and records, provided the full range of Arabic music—from Egyptian classical to Algerian rock. He also sold lutes, zithers, and other distinctive instruments of the region.

Hummus and Tabbouleh: Middle Eastern Food Comes of Age

Sarkis Colombosian and his son Bob drove their small paneled truck to Atlantic Avenue in the 1950s looking for prospects for a new product, bottles of yogurt from their Wild Rose Dairy in Andover, Massachusetts. Their expeditions were risky—they were peddling a strange product that was unlicensed in New York State.

The Colombosians, who managed to sign up Sahadi's and other Lebanese groceries, had shrewdly chosen their market. At that time, yogurt was a "hidden secret only the Middle Eastern community knew about," Charlie Sahadi observed.

Rose and Sarkis Colombosian, a young Armenian couple, fled their Turkish persecutors in 1917. After a short stay in Chicago, they journeyed to Lawrence, Massachusetts, a woolen mill town in northeastern Massachusetts with a rapidly growing Middle Eastern population.

Syrians, Lebanese, and Armenians were the latest in a long line of set-tlers—English, Irish, French Canadians, Italians—to arrive there.

In 1929, on the eve of the Depression, the Colombosians left Lawrence and bought a small dairy farm in nearby North Andover, Massachusetts. The family and their two young sons, John and Bob, began scratching out a living. Rose and Sarkis brewed yogurt, a staple of the Armenian diet. A pan of milk was usually warming on the stove. The family made *ayran*, a cooling drink with counterparts throughout the Middle East, from their homemade *matzoon*.

The Colombosians stumbled into the yogurt business. They churned out more milk than they could sell or use at home. They de-cided to use the extra to make yogurt that they could market on their milk route. It became a handy way to eke out extra income during the Depression. "Survival. That's what it was all about," Bob Colombosian recalled. "You made $10 a week and you were doing great."

The family cooked up their yogurt cottage-industry style. First in their kitchen and then in their backyard garage, they heated the milk in bottles over a wood stove. They filled the quart glass containers by hand and labeled them "Colombo" because, as Bob tells it, "nobody could pronounce our name."

In horse-drawn wagons the Wild Rose Dairy owners peddled their product. They soon developed a busy trade among the Syrians, Lebanese, Greeks, and Armenians who lived in Lowell, Haverhill, and other nearby towns. Immigrant families, many of whom worked in the mills, no longer had the time to make yogurt the traditional way. The Colombosians offered them an item "as cheap to buy as to make," Bob says.

These immigrants all came from societies fond of yogurt. Their lands had been conquered by the Turks, who spread cultured-milk dishes throughout their empire. In fact, "yogurt" derives from the Turkish word "to thicken." The nomadic herdsmen who grazed cat-tle, sheep, and goats on the barren steppes of Central Asia discov-ered that by fermenting milk they could more easily preserve and transport it.

Levantines also had their own yogurt traditions. They used it as a side dish with pilaf and as a dressing for sharply seasoned fried egg-plant or zucchini. Yogurt enriched stews and casseroles. Accented with garlic, mint, or dill, it metamorphosed into a tangy dip or salad.

☆ ☆

From households, the Colombosians turned to groceries. Their first customers were Middle Eastern shops. "The only place you could sell it was at the ethnic stores in the beginning," Bob said. They made a breakthrough in Watertown, a small town near Boston with a large Armenian colony. The Mugars, Armenian merchants who owned two stores there, began ordering their yogurt and two new products, *lab-neh,* a tangy cheese prepared from strained yogurt, and an Armenian string cheese, from their fellow ethnics in the 1940s. Star Markets, a Massachusetts supermarket chain that the Mugars would build, con-tinued to carry Colombo.

Even as it was edging into the commercial mainstream, the business was still a primitive operation. Their "homestead plant," as Bob called it, turned out yogurt in small lots that sold for twenty-five cents a quart wholesale throughout the 1950s. Rose and Sarkis only reluc-tantly installed bottling machinery and incubating equipment.

The public was still wary of the strange, unappetizing product. Even people from his hometown, Bob said, were repelled: "What the hell is that yucky stuff you sell?" neighbors asked him.

Yogurt's reputation would change. Dr. Gaylord Hauser, a popular medical writer, helped transform yogurt from alien custard to health food. In an October 1950 *Reader's Digest* article, the physician praised yogurt as a source of protein and touted it as a surefire way to "look younger and live longer." Health-food stores began selling yogurt soaps, creams, tablets, and cultures for making yogurt. Early converts discovered Colombo in these shops.

The health-food stores paved the way for Colombo to enter the su-permarket. The company soon dominated the plain-yogurt market, but the product's sour taste still hindered mass appeal. Consumers wanted more healthful food but had not lost their sweet tooth. "American people like a lot of sugar," Bob Colombosian learned.

Bob and his brother, John, who took over the company after Sarkis's death in 1966, overhauled their brand. They sweetened the top of the yogurt and put various fruit preserves in the bottom. Shoppers, Bob hoped, would no longer "spit it out when they took a bite." A new line of fruit flavors was introduced in 1971. Sales soared "like a rocket," he said.

But the dairy's outmoded operation could not keep up with rising demand for the product. "I'm not going to be doing this for the rest of my life in my backyard," Bob remembered thinking. In 1970 the dairy moved out of the backyard and into a modern plant in Methuen.

The company generated $1 million in sales in the factory's first year. Consumers warmed to the product, which was no longer sold in bottles but in blue and white paper cups. Desperately short of capital needed to succeed in a mass market, the brothers started looking for a backer. In 1977 they sold the business to Bon Grain, a French conglomerate. General Mills, which now owns Colombo, acquired the firm in 1993.

Bob Colombosian marvels at the changes in yogurt he has seen. The once rough-hewn *matzoon* has become a supermarket snack. The developments have been so dramatic, his father "would roll over in his grave." Bob, who now helps his daughter run a yogurt and ice cream shop in Salem, has not changed his own tastes. He still prefers his yogurt "plain."

☆ ☆

"Hummus and tabbouleh are sold in every deli in America," merchant Charlie Sahadi observed. By the 1980s, Middle Eastern food was becoming desirable, even fashionable, and ethnic business owners were changing their market strategy. Charlie, who had taken over the shop from his father, set out to transform a "foreign food store" into an "international" establishment that would attract both an immigrant and a sophisticated clientele. The time was ripe. Affluent newcomers were renovating the brownstones of Brooklyn Heights and Cobble Hill, neighborhoods close to Atlantic Avenue. He courted this population aggressively, tripling the size of the shop and filling it with a cornucopia of goods—twenty-seven brands of olive oil, as well as vinegars, teas, chocolates, preserves, and biscuits.

The emporium offers a tantalizing display of Middle Eastern goods. It carries ninety types of dried fruits and nuts—pistachios and pine nuts, Egyptian dates and extra large Turkish apricots. Brand-name products such as Casbah pilaf, Apollo filo dough, Near East couscous, and Sahadi's own brand of tahini, honey, cucumber pickles, and halvah fill the shelves. His deli markets tabbouleh, grape leaves, hummus, and other prepared foods to busy shoppers.

Sahadi is attentive to the changing tastes of his increasingly diverse ethnic customers. A new wave of Arabic immigrants—Moroccans, Egyptians, Yemenites, Palestinians—and an outpouring of Muslim refugees from Syria and Lebanon have invigorated Atlantic Avenue. The store offers them pickled turnips and fig jam from Lebanon, *mloukhiyeh,* a spinachlike leaf used in soup, from Egypt, and *zaatar,* a mélange of thyme, sesame, and sumac, from Jordan. Sahadi packs the grocery with brand names familiar to the immigrants, which, in the early days, had been difficult to import: Cortes orange water, Najjar coffee with cardamom, Karam *lebany* (a yogurt cheese) in oil, with mint or with thyme.

Sahadi attributes his success to "marrying the ethnic and specialty customer." He teases upscale buyers with a display of McCann's Irish oatmeal—"low fat, low sodium, low cholesterol," hoping that they will also sample some olives. A Middle Eastern customer searching for a special brand of imported grape leaves may leave with a bag of dried cranberries. Both immigrant and nonimmigrant are bolder today. "Everyone's willing to try someone else's food," he says.

Business is booming. On a Friday afternoon, shoppers, who must take a numbered ticket to be served, jam the store, which is brimming with barrels of briny olives, coolers of Mediterranean cheeses, bags of sumac, whole thyme, and other fragrant Middle Eastern spices. Sahadi's has become almost as fashionable as Balducci's, New York City's Italian gourmet supermarket. Charlie has realized his commercial dreams: "We went from being an ethnic, Middle Eastern store to a specialty food store featuring Middle Eastern food."

The food fashions that have made the business so successful amuse Charles Sahadi. "Today they talk the Mediterranean diet, but the Mediterranean diet has been our diet all our life," he says. Food writers and nutritionists are urging their audience to eat more bulgur, chickpeas, olive oil, and other Middle Eastern food.

Joe Shuad, who ran the nut business after his father's death, attracted a following from the "health and natural-food people." California longevity centers lauded his chickpeas, which were roasted and made into flour, for their "100 percent protein content." Joe developed a powdered drink made from a chickpea base for the Pritikin diet program.

The Sahadi marketing machine disseminates Middle Eastern food across the country. The wholesaler supplies "Mediterranean" groceries, mostly mom-and-pop stores in twenty-six states, from a mammoth list of more than 900 items. He offers them cucumber pickles, pistachio delight, and other Sahadi brand-name items and distributes rose water, dried okra, and pumpkin seeds, as well as a wealth of other domestic and imported items. These shops, in turn, spread the cuisine's lore to cosmopolitan customers.

Sahadi tries to shape his clients in his own image. Omar Elshafey, the Egyptian proprietor of a mini mart in my neighborhood, is a Sahadi disciple. He is awed by this "big, big guy" and models the "look of my store" on the Brooklyn bazaar.

Elshafey's wares reflect the Sahadi imprint. Three kinds of crumbly halvah—plain, pistachio, and chocolate—are displayed on the deli counter. A refrigerated case is stocked with *haloumi*, a salty Cypriot cheese, several varieties of olives, hummus, and *baba ghanouj*.

Sahadi nudges his clients to reach out to a cosmopolitan clientele: "They have to broaden their customer base. You're not getting enough outsiders to try the food." Omar is listening. A shelf of bottles of Colavita olive oil stands out amid the clutter of bags of rice and chick-peas, containers of apricots, raisins, carob, and figs, and the racks of Arabic videos. The Egyptian retailer buys his olive oil from the Brooklyn magnate.

☆ ☆

The popularity of Middle Eastern food has also changed the old-fash-ioned lunch counter. At George's Townhouse, an eatery in Washing-ton's Georgetown neighborhood, locals are savoring falafel while Lebanese, Kuwaitis, and other immigrants are discovering Philly cheese steaks and their tantalizing toppings of hot peppers, fried onions, and green peppers.

A natural showman, George Rababy, the Lebanese owner who calls himself the "king of falafel," plays to his audience. "If it is not fresh cooked in front of you, it's not falafel," he insists. He serves me a plate of tart olives and slices of red turnip that have been marinated in beet juice, hot pepper, vinegar, and salt to sharpen my appetite. Waiting for my falafel, I watch the performance.

George dips what looks like an ice cream scoop into the falafel mix and drops a patty into the fryer. Moments later he takes the fritter out, making sure that it is crunchy and moist. After letting it sit for a few minutes, he mashes the falafel on pocketless pita and garnishes it with lettuce, tomato, parsley, and turnips. He rolls up the pita to make a sandwich and squirts creamy sesame tahini sauce on it. As I bite into the falafel, I experience a burst of pungent flavor. I drink a glass of lemonade, flavored with orange blossom syrup, a fragrance cherished in the Middle East. After the protein-packed meal, George assures me, I will not be hungry for the rest of the day.

A stickler for tradition, George makes his falafel from scratch. He is contemptuous of the powdered mixes other restaurants use. The main ingredients, two-thirds fava beans and one-third chickpeas, soak in water for two days. George grinds the beans into a paste and seasons them with cumin, red pepper, and garlic. True falafel, he points out, has a bite. "If it's not hot, don't eat it." For added seasoning, he sprinkles parsley and coriander from a leafy pile on his basement worktable into the mix. George insists that falafel defies mass production. Making the croquette, he emphasizes, requires a deft hand. "Everybody has a different touch."

Growing up in Beirut, George soaked up the falafel tradition. He absorbed the culture by eating at restaurants like Saoun and Arax that specialized in the product. "Every day I used to go to eat falafel," he remembers. He savors the memory of a grand falafel house—a "hundred seats wide"—that offered customers a vast array of peppers, pickles, turnips, tomatoes, and other condiments for their sandwiches.

The history of falafel, a snack of ancient lineage, George says, goes back to the days of the pharaohs. The name most likely derives from the Arabic word for spicy, *mefelfel*. The Copts, an Egyptian Christian sect, claim to have invented the *ta'amia*, the fava-bean fritter that is parent to the falafel. During Lent, they ate it as a substitute for meat. The "poor man's meat" grew into a street food that was hawked by Egyptian vendors. It was soon transplanted to Lebanon and other Arab countries. The Lebanese created a hybrid, combining chickpeas with fava beans.

The Israelis also put their own stamp on the falafel. They borrowed the dish from Sephardic immigrants from Morocco, Yemen, and Syria. Israeli falafel, which is made exclusively from chickpeas, is enjoyed in restaurants whose salad bars dispense eggplant, cucumbers, tomatoes, and other relishes. Vendors often spark falafel with *zhug*, a hot pepper sauce from Yemen laced with cloves, cinnamon, and cardamom.

☆ ☆

The journey of the future falafel impresario began in Beirut in 1974. Fearful that civil war would soon erupt, the police lieutenant's son took his wife, Nawal, and two young children to Akron, Ohio. Two of his cousins owned taverns, a business in the Midwest that attracted

Lebanese Christians. George decided against the bar business and left for Washington, where friends offered to help him find a job.

George, who had trained in French and Arabic cooking at a Beirut hotel school, struggled to gain a foothold in a city that didn't recognize his culinary credentials. He found a job at La Grande Scene, the Kennedy Center's rooftop restaurant. Eager for experience, he moved on to other restaurant jobs. "I was trying to learn every kind of food," he said.

He capped his American apprenticeship with a six-year stint at Bacchus, a sophisticated Lebanese restaurant, where he picked up some important lessons about the American palate. Surprisingly, Americans liked their dishes spicier than the Lebanese did. They were also intensely curious about food. "They love to hear explanations about the food," George said. "After this, when it sounds interesting to them, they love to try it."

Searching for a "busy place to show my experience," George chanced on Jack's Steaks, a luncheonette, for sale right off Georgetown's heavily trafficked M Street. On May 28, 1988, he took over the modest shop, which had a small lunch counter, a few stools, a tiny kitchen, and a little upstairs dining room.

For the first month, George kept Jack's old short-order menu, but he soon added falafel and a few other Arabic items to the list of sandwiches, subs, and cheese steaks. He encouraged customers who asked for a tuna sandwich "to take some falafel."

Falafel caught fire, and with this drawing card, he built up a Lebanese snack bar. He served a pita sandwich that the Syrians and Lebanese called an *arus* (bride). It is spread with *labneh,* the yogurt cheese that tastes like a marriage of cream cheese and sour cream; the cheese is sprinkled with mint and drizzled with olive oil. He sold lemony grape leaves; kibbe, bulgur-based snacks shaped like small footballs; hummus; *baba ghanouj;* and *shawarma,* a Middle Eastern gyro of pressed tenderloin dressed with tahini, sumac, and parsley.

A varied cast of characters visits the Townhouse—Lebanese doctors and other professionals, Georgetown nightclubbers, and college students from the Persian Gulf, where George's reputation has spread, come to order dinner or carry out. Two Ethiopians venture in for falafel, a dish they had only recently discovered. A young Turkish man asks for a dish of yogurt to go with the lunch special, a beef and okra stew. A new college student, from one of the Arab countries, purchases a bottle of orange blossom water for her kitchen.

Culinary traditions intermingle in the lunchroom. Middle Eastern customers have found a way to give their cheese steaks a Levantine touch: They ask George to douse them with tahini.

"Cheezborga, Cheezborga, Cheezborga, No Coke, Pepsi": The Greek Restaurant Odyssey

Emigration agents began to scour the country, exciting the imagination of the peasants as to the glories and opportunities of America.

Henry Pratt Fairchild
(*Greek Immigration to the United States*, 1911)

From Red Hots to Snack Shops

THE GREEK RESTAURANT ODYSSEY began in the late nineteenth and early twentieth centuries when waves of Hellenic immigrants cascaded onto American shores. The enterprises they launched were the ancestors of today's diners and coffee shops.

The diaspora (a Greek word), which carried the adventurous people throughout the Mediterranean in the ancient epoch of empire, was founding a new colony. From the time of Alexander the Great through their colonization by the Turks, Greek immigrants engaged in shipping, banking, and business. The Greeks occupied the commercial positions in Egypt, Romania, and Syria that the locals rejected. In Constantinople itself, the seat of the Ottoman empire, the Turks permitted the Greeks their commercial pursuits.

The migration to industrial America was a journey of masses, primarily of villagers, single men leaving the countryside behind, in search of fabled opportunities. Between 1900 and 1920, 400,000 immigrants poured in. Many of them hailed from Sparta and other communities in the Peloponnesus, the country's poor southern region.

These sojourners had the most limited objectives. As soon as they saved enough money, they planned to return to their villages. They worked feverishly so that one day they could buy land and invest in business.

Above all, emigration was a family project in which older sons and fathers were sent off in behalf of their clan. Families backed their males by mortgaging or selling land and borrowing money. Some promised to pay back the loans from the immigrants' future earnings.

Labor contractors enticed immigrants with tales of fortunes to be made in America. Agents for railroads, factories, and shoeshine businesses traveled to Greek villages to corral a labor force. They coaxed parents into releasing their sons, with families mortgaging their land as security.

☆ ☆

The newcomers sought out the cities, not the countryside. Textile mills and shoe factories in New England, mines in the West, and plants in New York and Philadelphia were magnets for the new immigrants. Chicago, America's oldest Greek colony, attracted the most settlers. A combination railroad center, commercial and shipping metropolis, and jumping-off point for jobs in the West, the heartland city had drawing power. By 1910, 15,000 Greeks had made it their home.

The Greek pioneers carved out an enclave, "Greektown," a densely packed commercial and residential zone on Chicago's West Side. The triangular-shaped area around Halsted Street was called the Delta because it resembled the Greek letter.

The newcomers tried to re-create a semblance of their homeland. Holy Trinity Church, which displayed a double cross as a symbol of orthodoxy, was the community's fulcrum. The *koinotis,* the church's paying members, was Greektown's most tightly bound body. Newspapers, schools, and ethnic associations kept the ties to the homeland alive.

Groceries, clothing stores, dry goods stores, and restaurants created a bustling commercial life. Edward Steiner, a writer who visited the neighborhood, was struck by the Hellenic feel of a food shop: "There are dried vegetables whose present form does not betray their natural shape, but which taste luscious, because the flavor of the native soil clings to them; fish, dried, pickled and preserved in some form, and cheese made from the milk of goats whose horns butted broken vases instead of modern tin cans. The smells seem ancient, too, but in these the Greek revels, and here he is at home."

The Greek bank, a combination steamship ticket office, notary public, and employment agency, connected settlers to their villages. It was where they came to negotiate tickets and papers for incoming relatives. The bank sent the immigrants' obligatory payments home to relatives—the Greeks in this era surpassed all ethnic groups in remittances.

Lonely bachelors congregated in the many *kaffenia* (coffeehouses) that lined Halsted Street. In 1910 more than twenty such businesses—Greek transplants with evocative names like Acropolis, Paradisos, Arcadia—were up and running. Popular gathering places after work and on the weekend, each coffeehouse attracted its own clientele—usually men from the same district in Greece.

The *kaffenia* served strong coffee, tea, cider, ice cream, and pastries like baklava in modest surroundings—tables, chairs, pictures of Greek heroes or battle scenes on the wall. The "dark and mustached sons of Hellas," as one writer described them, smoked Turkish pipes and drank endless cups of coffee. The immigrants came to talk, to regale each other with stories of Greece and tales of their new land.

They gambled and played cards—pinochle or thirty-one—tipping the owner to indulge their pastime. The coffeehouses sometimes provided entertainment; customers danced to *bouzouki* music or watched belly dancers perform.

Greek sociability precipitated a puritanical backlash from the city fathers. In 1927, Chicago Mayor Carter Harrison II damned the *kaffenia* for fostering "vice" and threatened to levy a tax on them. Police pounced on them in gambling raids, prompting such newspaper headlines as "Acropolis Closed" and "Paradise Is Raided."

☆ ☆

Full of this pride and confidence in themselves, they are nevertheless ready to blacken our boots for ten cents, and they do it remarkably well, displacing negroes and Italians, until later, they open stores and sell American candies to an undiscriminating public, hungry for cheap sweets. No labor is too hard for them, although they prefer to stand by the counter.

Edward Steiner
(*On the Trail of the Immigrant*, 1906)

The immigrants were not content to huddle in Greektowns. These ethnic islands were too confining for the urban mariners, whose thirst for adventure sent them journeying into the mainstream.

Greeks quickly grew restless with their first jobs, hard labor on railroads, in steel mills and meat-packing plants, and on construction gangs. They bridled at working for a boss, especially one who was not a kinsman. The immigrants looked on jobs as a way station, as a first step to their ancient dream of self-employment.

The budding entrepreneurs fixed on trade, no matter how petty, as their means of ascent. They searched for a niche in the marketplace and burrowed into it. Hawking flowers, fruit, and candy from trays, baskets, and pushcarts was a popular venture. Start-up costs were low, use of English was minimal, and the lure of future gains was enticing. They also hoped to parlay their gains into a larger business. Trade had powerful appeal to immigrants gathering a nest egg for their return home.

Many peddlers began as virtual indentured servants, working off the passage money that labor bosses had advanced them. The apprentices put up with brutal hours and atrocious pay to learn the ropes. After the young initiates paid off their debts and gained sufficient experience, they often went out on their own.

The trade was hazardous. Chicago police harassed produce sellers, forcing them to pay bribes or risk arrest. In 1908 they arrested nearly 900 vendors for violations of city ordinances. Established businessmen, some of them Greeks, pressured the Chicago city council to tax peddlers if they sold their goods in the streets or alleys.

To succeed, the peddlers had to vanquish their competition. In Chicago, Greeks battled the Italians, earlier arrivals who had established a niche in the fruit business, for control of the trade. The Mediterranean rivals felt intense animosity for each other: "There is a bitter feud between these two races, as deeply seated as the enmity that engendered the Graeco-Roman Wars," the *Chicago Tribune* reported in 1895. By 1900 the Greeks had achieved supremacy in retail and wholesale produce.

In other cities, their commercial prowess gave Greeks the edge. The intrepid traders searched out new markets in New York City, while the Italian merchants clung to their ethnic neighborhoods. "They are also more adroit because of greater exposure in foreign countries," writer Konrad Bercovici observes of Greek fruit dealers in New York City in the 1920s. "You will seldom find Italian stores away from the Italian districts. But the Greeks avoid their own districts. Their people are too economical. . . . There is no profit in selling to one's own people, who know the exact value of the thing they buy."

☆ ☆

Vending was a jumping-off point for larger retailing and wholesaling enterprises. Christos Tsakonas, the Spartan fruit and candy magnate, exemplified the entrepreneurial dream.

Tsakonas, who grew up in a poor peasant family in the village of Tsintzina, left home at fourteen. He tried his luck working in *kaffenia* in Athens and Piraeus and moved on to Alexandria, a popular destination for migrating Greeks, in the early 1870s. Unsuccessful as a money changer, the restless wanderer fixed his eyes on America.

Tsakonas arrived in New York City in 1873 and soon began peddling candy from a street-corner pushcart. Hungry for new opportunities, he headed for California but landed in Chicago instead, where he again picked up the peddling trade. He turned enough profits hawking fruits that he was able to return to Tsintzina in 1875 to pay off family debts.

Tsakonas brought five young villagers back with him to Chicago. They were the first in a stream of Tsintzinians who rushed into the Midwestern city during the 1870s and 1880s. The "Columbus of Sparta" preached the gospel of economic advancement to his disciples. Like Tsakonas, many of them sought their fortune in the fruit and candy trade.

Tsakonas, for unexplained reasons, left Chicago for Milwaukee in 1882. After opening fruit and candy shops there, he wandered through the blooming industrial towns of western Pennsylvania and eastern Ohio, setting up more stores and placing Tsintzinian pioneers at their helm.

He stitched together ten shops to form the Greek American Fruit Company. In the mid-1880s, he linked his enterprises with Tsintzinian fruit suppliers in California and Hawaii. California merchants imported pineapples and bananas from Hawaii and shipped them to their compatriots in Chicago. These wholesalers sent the fruit on to shops in Pennsylvania and Ohio.

Greek merchants prospered in the candy trade, a business they eventually monopolized. The shops made and sold American sweets—caramels, hand-dipped chocolates—not Greek confections, and carried candy bars, tobacco, and chewing gum. In Chicago, the "Acropolis" of the business, dealers were running more than 900 shops in 1906.

They skillfully picked locations throughout downtown, near the main stores and movie theaters. "Practically every busy corner of

Chicago is occupied by a Greek candy store," cheered the newspaper *Hellenikos Astir* in 1904. Chicagoans flocked to the stores, Jimmy Mezilson, the son of a shop owner, remembers, because they were "social gathering places."

Chicago also became the capital of candy wholesaling. Wholesalers sent out salesmen to supply shops in smaller communities, often run by Tsintzinian dealers who learned the trade in Chicago. Their suppliers, also compatriots, helped them with the capital and know-how needed to get established. Although miles away, shops with names like Sugarland and Candy Land in places such as Akron, Ohio, Ithaca, New York, and Morgantown, West Virginia, were tied ethnically and economically to their Chicago sponsors.

Ice cream was an integral part of the candy business. From marble fountains in ornately decorated shops, merchants whipped up ice cream sodas. Capitalizing on their ties to the booming fruit trade, they mixed cherries, pineapples, and other "fancy" fruits in sundaes, a Greek creation according to immigrant folklore.

Some confectioneries blossomed into larger enterprises. Leo Stefanos, an immigrant who opened the Dove Candies Shop in Chicago in 1939, dreamed up the Dove bar. He invented the dessert after experimenting with hand-dipping ice cream bars into a bowl of bittersweet warm chocolate. Mike Stefanos, who took over the company from his late father, remembers the tedious trial and error of the venture: "There's a lot of things in the coatings. All the things came from burning our hands in the chocolate all these years." Dove grew from a neighborhood store to a company manufacturing an "adult super-premium dessert."

Thomas Andreas Carvelas, another ice cream magnate, started out as a Studebaker test driver in Yonkers, New York. He invented a machine to make soft ice cream and, in 1935, bought an old truck with $15 borrowed from his future wife from which to sell his product. The Carvel ice cream empire of franchises using the entrepreneur's equipment and marketing his wares developed from this early venture.

The confectioners enthusiastically embraced the culture on which their livelihood depended. Viewed warily in this xenophobic age, they were determined to endear themselves to their clientele. The Greek Confectioners Association urged its members to blend in: "Let us Americanize ourselves. We make our bread and butter in America. We deal and trade with American people; we breathe free American air. Let us adopt the best they have, and let us unite ourselves with the best friends that Greeks could ever wish for. America and Americans are our best friends and protectors."

The economic environment, once so favorable to the candy business, eventually soured. By the early 1930s, mainstream drugstores with soda fountains and five-and-dimes were supplanting the Greek candy store. With the end of Prohibition, some Chicago Greeks began turning their shops into taverns.

☆ ☆

In peddling, Greeks found a handy route into the restaurant business. Outside factory gates and on the streets of the Loop, Chicago's downtown, vendors in the early 1900s hawked red hots—the name still used today for hot dogs—and tamales from pushcarts and lunch wagons. Cities clamped down on the street trade through health codes and other regulations: Chicago Mayor Carter Harrison instituted a ban on food vending in 1927.

But the entrepreneurs' ambitions were not easily thwarted. John Raklios, a Greek immigrant in Chicago, tenaciously climbed the ladder to become a restaurant titan. Raklios, who journeyed to the Midwest at the turn of the century, started out peddling chestnuts and bananas. Arrested for vending without a license, he scraped together enough money to open a fruit stand. Soon after, he jumped from the fruit business to selling hamburgers in Chicago's burlesque district. He ultimately acquired his first restaurant, the launching pad for a food empire that by 1930 had thirty eateries. Raklios scouted locations for his corner shops with a keen eye, staying up all night counting pedestrian and automobile traffic.

These masters of the fast sell easily transferred their skills to the quick-order lunchroom, an apter description than restaurant. Family members banded together pooling capital and labor. Sometimes owners mortgaged the family farm in Greece to raise funds. The businesses provided jobs as countermen and dishwashers to other immigrants, who in time often left to start their own eateries.

This entrepreneurial vitality produced a burgeoning restaurant business. Greeks were running a third of Chicago's lunchrooms in 1919. In Manhattan they owned 107 food establishments in 1907. The Greeks had even penetrated the West Coast market—they had 564 restaurants in San Francisco in 1923.

The immigrants concentrated on pursuing the American trade. Chicago operators located near factories to attract the crowds of shift workers. Restaurant owners also set up many of their lunchrooms in the Loop, a good location for snaring downtown workers. The "snack shops," Chicago lingo for what New Yorkers now call "coffee shops," were purveyors of quick meals to people on the run.

The lunchroom trade craved hot dogs, not hamburgers, and consumed tamales. Instead of bagels or muffins, customers bought pie and coffee. Tasty pies were the restaurants' drawing card. Countermen chanted "stamberry pie, peaca pie, happula pie, pinehappula pie" in Chicago novelist Harry Petrakis's rendition.

For all their efforts to please, the Greek restaurateurs encountered intense suspicion. Many Americans looked down on businessmen who had dark, Mediterranean complexions. A restaurant in Santa Rosa, California, reassured potential customers in a newspaper ad: "John's Restaurant. Pure American. No Rats, No Greeks."

Greek restaurant owners tried to assuage the public's fears. The immigrants proclaimed themselves reliable and loyal Americans. Many owners dropped the foreign-sounding names of their restaurants. The American Association of Greek Restaurant Keepers, founded in 1919, set up a program to encourage members to become U.S. citizens. To promote a more wholesome image, the group prodded restaurant owners to follow the most rigorous sanitation standards.

Diners and Coffee Shops

By the end of World War II, the first generation of Greek restaurant owners was aging and had no obvious successors. Their children had loftier, white-collar ambitions. In time new tides of immigration replenished the Greek food business. The U.S. government lifted immigration restrictions, which opened the door to 70,000 Greeks between 1945 and 1965. Some arrived in less conventional ways. Over 80,000 Greeks jumped ship in American ports between 1957 and 1974, sociologist Charles Moskos points out.

Encouraged by the 1965 immigration law, which promoted family reunion, Greeks streamed in to join their kin. This infusion—15,000 a year between 1966 and 1971—steadily enlarged the Hellenic community. Mothers, sisters, and daughters changed the balance of the once largely masculine enclaves.

Like the Greek pioneers, the new arrivals gravitated to the food business. "When you first jump off the ship, the first thing you need is food. In order to eat you have to work in a restaurant." So Marios Christodoulides, the Greek Cypriot manager of a Queens, New York, restaurant supplier, explains this Greek affinity for the restaurant business. An earlier generation had already proven that the restaurant could be a profitable enterprise. "You're not going to start a plumbing business," Christodoulides continues.

Unlike their cautious predecessors, some of the new arrivals chose to market their own cuisine. Chicago's Greektown, most of which had been demolished to make room for the Eisenhower freeway, became a commercial district, sprouting with restaurants and nightclubs. Twenty Chicago restaurants offered an extensive Greek menu in 1978. The city had only one such restaurant in 1966.

No longer an immigrant oasis, the Delta lured tourists and adventurous Chicagoans eager to sample the Greek experience. The Halsted Street merchants manufactured a raucous atmosphere of *bouzouki* music, dancing waiters, and spirited ouzo drinking. Waiters carried platters of flaming *saganaki*, fried *gravera* cheese doused in cognac—a creation of Chicago restaurateurs, not a Greek import.

Proprietors introduced their guests to a culinary world that stretched far beyond egg lemon soup, grape leaves, roast lamb, and other standbys. I discovered such tangy dishes as *skordalia*, a bread-based dip laced with garlic and sharpened with vinegar, and *tzatziki*, a blend of yogurt and cucumbers also pungent with garlic, at my favorite Washington restaurant, the now-shuttered Greek Port. Despina Nomikos, the Washington eatery's effusively hospitable cook, complemented the starters with crisply fried eggplant and zucchini.

Recent immigrants like Despina and her husband Moskos were suspicious of adulterated "Greek-American" food. Despina insisted on preparing the "original" moussaka, not the precooked version that distributors sold. With a small touch, she invested a conventional dish with novelty and authenticity. She transformed a Greek salad by sprinkling fresh dill on it.

The new Greektowns sold an abundance of goods more extensive than those available in earlier settlements. In Astoria, the Queens, New York, neighborhood that surpassed Chicago as the capital of Greek America after World War II, residents and weekend shoppers could purchase videos and newspapers, search for their favorite olives, cheeses, and honeys, and enjoy the pleasures of *tavernas*, nightclubs, and *kaffenia*. To satisfy their customers' wants, Astoria's shops cast a wide net. Fish stores sold *barbuni* (red mullet), and butcher shops displayed sheep heads.

☆ ☆

Most of the newcomers, however, were attracted to the American food business. Greeks spotted an opening in the Northeastern diner business in the mid-1950s. Irish, German, and Jewish owners, whose children had little appetite for the business, were selling out. Greeks began taking their places.

The diner was not originally an ethnic business. A vintage American institution, it descended from the lunch wagons that their owners wheeled about in 1870s Rhode Island selling evening meals to workers. As diner consultant Richard Gutman points out, the diner was "originally open to people from all walks of life." The Greeks took this vehicle of upward mobility and put their unmistakable stamp on it.

In their heyday, the 1960s and 1970s, diners appealed to immigrants who had entrepreneurial dreams and little capital. Seeing a way to expand their own business, diner manufacturers and restaurant suppliers were ready to lend a hand. They often advanced 75 percent of the down payment, says Harold Kullman, who runs the New Jersey–based Kullman Dining Car Company. Kullman, whose father, a Russian Jewish immigrant, founded the company after working as an accountant for an early diner builder, observes that diners are the "only business you can get into with such a minute amount of money," making them an irresistible bargain. "When I started, diners were sold by the running foot like boats," he told writer Peter Genovese. For "sixteen thousand dollars, you could buy a diner."

The luncheonette, Kullman points out, was a popular route into the diner business. From there, the operator might move to a "starter diner," a simple lunch-counter establishment with a grill and open kitchen. A core staff of chef, baker, and "front of the house" manager ran the rudimentary enterprise.

Diner owners graduated from basic businesses to more spacious suburban and highway establishments. These restaurants boasted their own parking lots, separate dining rooms, and even waiters. A closed-in kitchen replaced the open grill.

Once Greeks established a beachhead in the industry, they extended job opportunities to friends and relations. From lowly diner jobs, they began their ascent up the ladder. Consultant Gutman describes the diner saga as a "Horatio Alger story": "I can't tell you the number of times the dishwasher ends up owning the place."

☆ ☆

The career of Jerry Vallianos epitomized the path of the Greek diner owner. After jumping ship in 1939 and serving in the army, he started working for his uncle, who owned the Garden State Restaurant, a diner in downtown Camden, New Jersey, in 1946. Starting as a dishwasher, he was promoted to short-order cook after only a few months. Shortly thereafter, he was elevated to chef, and he took the reins of the restaurant from his uncle in 1948.

Then, the restless entrepreneur left the Garden State in 1954 to undertake another venture. He leased a twenty-four-hour diner in the Fairview, New Jersey, bus terminal, a restaurant known affectionately as "Shorty's" (after its owner). Seven years later, Jerry moved again to take over a diner he picked up in a bankruptcy sale. Owned by a Polish businessman, the Fair-Lynn, down the street from Shorty's, was a stainless-steel diner on the outskirts of Camden a quarter mile from the Fairview. It had been built by the Kullman company. Jerry discovered several woks among the diner's kitchen equipment—apparently it had served both Chinese and American food.

Peering at his watch one day in his lawyer's office, Jerry decided to rename the diner the Elgin. The restaurant in its early days catered to a solid blue-collar clientele. Camden, a smokestack Delaware River town, was booming because of growing companies like Campbell's Soup and RCA. The shipyards provided plentiful jobs. Jerry's son, George, remembers the factory workers who jammed the diner: "At 4:00 o'clock the whistle blew and this place filled up with guys with lunch pails." The Elgin's customers represented the ethnic mix of a city with sharply defined Polish, Italian, and Jewish neighborhoods.

George, who grew up helping out at the Elgin, chose a path very different from that of his self-taught father. After coming out of the Coast Guard, he decided to prepare himself for a restaurant career. He trained at the Culinary Institute of America in West Point, New York, then honed his skills in the restaurant of the Hyatt Hotel in Cherry Hill, New Jersey, where he learned all facets of the food business. George returned to the family business in 1976, where he gradually assumed more of the responsibilities for running the restaurant. Jerry

Vallianos died in 1982, and George's uncle, Spiro, who had been Jerry's partner, decided to retire.

In the early 1980s, when George took control of the Elgin, Camden's economy was beginning to fray. The closing of the Campbell's and RCA plants decimated the city's manufacturing base. The industrial shutdowns led to an exodus of workers and the middle class. Poor black and Hispanic families made up an ever-larger share of the city's thinning ranks.

The Elgin, George says, is an "economic barometer" of Camden. As the city changed, so did the profile of the diner's customers. White-collar workers from the government offices that opened across the street helped fill the void left by the disappearing blue-collar clientele. The diner also began drawing more minority customers.

☆ ☆

A mammoth menu, which offered a vast array of items from omelettes and pancakes to veal cutlets and pasta, was the diner's trademark. The Elgin's 1994 breakfast menu, which ran three pages, listed nine omelette choices, nine pancake combinations, and a potpourri of side orders, including lyonnais potatoes, scrapple, and kielbasa.

The diners dished up such standbys as liver and onions and meat-loaf, heavy meals to stoke the engines of truck drivers, construction workers, and factory hands who worked nearby. Customers drove to the diners hungering for comfort foods. "Where else do you go to get mashed potatoes and gravy?" asks the Elgin's George Vallianos rhetorically.

Diner menus have become interchangeable, builder Harold Kullman observes, as the fiercely competitive operators "copy from each other." "Everyone is always looking to see what the other guy is doing. When somebody puts something on the menu, it's like sending a telegram," notes Jimmy Dontis, a Brooklyn produce-company owner.

No item is too unusual for the diner menu. George Vallianos began offering grits to please black customers who grew up in the South.

Some Greek-owned coffee shops, a New York City variation on the diner, served blintzes for their Jewish clientele.

The diners have replaced the simpler sweets of the earlier Greek lunchrooms with more elaborate desserts. In New York City, decadent confections—napoleons, lemon meringue pies, cheesecakes—beckon customers from "show-off cases," the revolving display cases their Queens manufacturer, Traulsen and Company, has so aptly named.

The Greeks have also transformed the diner's exterior. During the 1970s, they developed an extravagant Mediterranean design to replace the restrained colonial architecture that had previously reigned. Inside, the restaurants displayed such lavish features as smoked mirrors and Greek statuary.

The ethnics had reshaped what Harold Kullman calls the "original short-order fast-food restaurant." They were reaching a wider audience on the highways of suburban America and were winning over a once wary public. The diners were erasing the stereotype of the slovenly restaurant owner. Greeks were exhibiting the values the culture most admired. As the Elgin's George Vallianos sums it up: "What sold the American people on the Greeks was their work ethic."

☆ ☆

The founders of New York City's coffee shops were adventurous Greeks who leaped boldly into new enterprises. Peter Zanikos, a fisherman's son from the island of Kyos, started out as a seaman making $30 a month. "As soon as the boat comes to America, I jump off," he says. "I jump off like crazy."

In the early 1960s, he took a job washing dishes and ultimately saved enough money to open his own coffee shop. From this building block, he assembled the Argo restaurant group, which at its peak consisted of twelve shops. For Zanikos, establishing a restaurant was a matter of pride: "So I told my wife: You're going to help me. I want to be somebody. I'm tired to be poor, me and my family."

He took advantage of the new immigration law to sponsor his mother, sister, and two brothers "from the other side." He installed his kin in his businesses and crows about his achievement: "These people 90 percent is here account of me."

Coffee-shop owners preferred to hire relatives and fellow ethnics rather than outsiders because they were more reluctant to complain about long hours and irregular schedules. For immigrants who aspired to opening their own restaurants, hardships were the price you paid to learn the business.

Like the diners, coffee shops were attractive to the Greeks because of their low start-up costs. Marcos Kalogeras, who owned New York City's Astro restaurant, reminisces about the ease of opening a business: "You go to the coffee man, he loan you $5,000 . . . the jukebox man $5,000. You go put $1,000 down and you have your own restaurant."

A network of suppliers grew up alongside the diners and coffee shops. Wholesalers, many Greeks themselves, supplied the restaurants with baked goods, fish, paper products, coffee, gyros, and other necessities.

The menu in these "mini diners" advertised a multitude of choices: fruits and juices, omelettes, seafood, Italian, club sandwiches, burgers. Homey items disappearing from other restaurants survived in the coffee shops. "They are the last holdouts for cantaloupe, cottage cheese, and Jell-O," restaurant historian Michael Batterberry observes. In addition, they usually offered a few Greek items—moussaka, souvlaki, Greek salad topped with crumbled feta. Rice pudding was a common dessert offering.

Like the Parthenon murals on the walls and the hanging vine leaves, the Greek dishes were exceptions to an American luncheonette theme. In Doreen Moses's affecting film *One on Every Corner*, a portrait of the coffee shops in New York City, a customer asks for "Greek lamb stew." The counterman replies: "For Greek lamb stew you have to go to Athens." The customers of diners and coffee shops wanted quick, convenient, familiar, and plentiful food, and the immigrant businessmen keenly adapted.

The coffee shop combines the intense sociability of Greek village culture with a brisk American pace. Hungry for connection, regulars are drawn to this island of warmth and hospitality in an impersonal city. Customers yearn for the familiar clatter, the rapid-fire order taking, and the wisecracking banter. *Saturday Night Live's* parody of the Greek countermen's patter—"Cheezborga, cheezborga, cheezborga, no Coke, Pepsi"—has become a permanent part of American folklore.

A specially designed paper coffee cup became the emblem of diners and coffee shops. The blue-and-white container, decorated on the sides with the frieze pattern of an amphora urn, was conceived by Leslie Buck, a salesman for Sherri, a Connecticut restaurant supplier. Captivated by the design he saw on a piece of Greek statuary, Buck convinced his company to put it on cups sold to Greek eateries. Sherri began distributing it in 1965. Restaurants in the New York, New Jersey, and southern Connecticut area devour 300 million cups a year. The "quintessential New York cup," as Lawrence Meadowcroft, Sherri's vice president for sales and marketing, calls it, has become a staple of television dramas. It is frequently seen in the hands of policemen and detectives on such shows as *NYPD Blue* and *Law and Order*.

The cups with their "we are happy to serve you" insignia have spread throughout New York's eateries. Whatever their nationality—Pakistani, Arab, Korean—newcomers to the food business are drawn to the universal container. Elisa Deixler, manager of Zahner's Cash and Carry, a restaurant supply store in Woodside, Queens, says demand for the product is insatiable: "Everyone wants that cup, no matter what language they speak. It's the only paper coffee cup we sell. Twenty-seven dollars a case, not including lids." Her associate, Marios Christodoulides, quips: "I don't see any with pyramids on it."

☆ ☆

New Greek immigrants in New York and New England were also attracted to the pizza trade. They plunged into a business considered the domain of the Italians. Once again the Greeks demonstrated their skill in reaching a wider market.

In Connecticut, the Italians, who began opening pizza shops in the 1920s, dominated the trade until the mid-1950s. From that time until the 1970s, Greek businessmen struck out for those parts of the state with the smallest Italian populations. When the Italians retired, their children and grandchildren, who stayed in the food business, abandoned pizzerias to go into full-service restaurants. As a result, a large chunk of the field was ceded to the scrappy Greeks, who swarmed into the state.

The Greeks developed a more efficient method of making the product. A Greek Albanian, who opened a pizza shop in New London in 1953, started preparing dough in advance and refrigerating it. When a pizza was ordered, he removed the pan, put on the topping, and baked the pie in the original container.

The pizza business became the portal for most Greeks entering the Connecticut job market. By the late 1970s, sociologist Lawrence Lovell-Troy points out, 76 percent of Greek families in the state worked in the business. A spiraling number of closely linked businesses sprang from an original enterprise run by one family member. A brother who owned a pizza shop would sponsor his sister, whose husband would open another shop and ask his brother to join him. The brother, in turn, would eventually start his own restaurant. Through ever-widening migration chains, Connecticut's pizza clans multiplied.

Ethnic ties were vital to Greeks opening a pizza business. A kinsman or fellow national would get an aspiring owner credit with suppliers of pizza ovens, food products, and paper supplies. One restaurant owner explains how he vouched for a former employee: "This guy, I helped him a lot. Because when he started, he couldn't speak good English. And I gave to him all my salesmen. . . . I gave my reputation to him. I was responsible. You know, if he don't pay, I pay."

☆ ☆

The diner business is changing. Like the pizzeria, the diner depended on an infusion of kinfolk. But the old immigration pipeline has been drying up. A new contingent of immigrants is not leaving Greece, and the children of restaurant owners are frequently reluctant to follow in their footsteps. "The American children of these Greek immigrants saw everything their fathers went through to run these businesses—incredibly long hours, lots of work, lots of sacrifice—and it simply doesn't appeal to them," says Peter Makrios, the publisher of *Estiator*, a magazine for Greeks in the food business. Entrepreneurial Greeks are tempted by other opportunities—in construction, flowers, and furs.

In New York City, Third World immigrants are more likely than Greeks to be working the dishwashing jobs, the traditional springboards into restaurant ownership. "It's not unlikely that one day a good deal of the business will be run by Mexicans," Makrios observes.

Recent ethnic groups have already invaded Greek turf. Their historic rivals, the Turks, have opened diners in New Jersey, sometimes erecting them out of former convenience stores. Korean delis in New York City have been taking customers away from the coffee shops. Philip Kalyvas, a New York City accountant, advises his Greek clients accordingly: "I tell them to put an ad in a Korean newspaper. The Koreans come with the money. They're walking with cash."

Marios Christodoulides, the Cypriot store manager, is accustomed to the constant upheaval in the restaurant business. "Whenever there's a problem in the world," he says, a flood of immigrants bursts into America. "The first thing they do is to start a restaurant."

Nostalgic for the diner's glory days, non-Greek businessmen are opening retro diners that attempt to duplicate its design and menu. They prepare old favorites like liver and onions with a new American gloss and introduce more sophisticated dishes. The owners of the A-1 Diner, a stainless-steel diner in Gardner, Maine, lured upscale customers with red pepper and leek lasagna and spicy polenta gratin.

The new owners have goals different from those of the Greeks. The earlier immigrants grabbed onto the diner as a means to get ahead.

The retro builders, says diner consultant Gutman, want to re-create a "bit of Americana." Some of them, he argues, feel that the diner "heritage has been robbed by the Greeks."

Some young Greek restaurateurs have committed themselves to the diner business while hoping to modernize it. Instead of the old seat-of-the-pants approach, the Elgin's George Vallianos favors "professional management." Many owners, he says, don't even know the exact quantity of food in their freezers. Wider use of computers to "control inventory" would promote diner efficiency.

Vallianos believes that even the cherished encyclopedic menu needs "trimming." Diners, he suggests, must adapt their menus to a changing clientele. His white-collar customers, who are more "fat-conscious," expect lighter dishes. The Elgin owner introduced a "petit menu" with smaller portions that his competitors have copied. The up-to-date diner will serve both Salisbury steak and skinless, boneless chicken breasts.

Other Greeks trade up and open steak houses or fancier full-service restaurants. The venues may be different, but their proprietors are no less food-obsessed, no less welcoming and effusive than the earlier owners of snack shops, coffee shops, diners, or pizzerias. An obituary for this lively ethnic niche would be premature.

CHAPTER 4

The "Heartburn of Nostalgia": Jewish Food in America

I love Jewish food, but when you eat it, seventy-two hours later, you're hungry again.

The late **Richard Shepard,**
New York Times reporter

Eating "Dairy" and "Delicatessen"

THE IMMIGRANT WOMEN "jabbered," "jostled," and "haggled," a reporter observed, amid the pushcarts and market stalls of the Hester Street market on New York's Lower East Side in the late nineteenth century. In this crucible of early Jewish immigrant culture, vendors peddled hot knishes, bagels, hot *arbes* (chickpeas), and horseradish. The eastern European newcomers, 1.6 million of whom poured into America between 1881 and 1910, avidly pursued food as a source of spiritual sustenance and reassuring nourishment.

Food businesses sprang up to cater to their distinctive tastes and religious strictures. Among the 631 merchants that historian Moses Rischin found selling their wares in the district's Tenth Ward in 1899 were 36 bakeries, 131 butcher shops, and 15 grape-wine dealers. There was an active trade in holiday items—five factories manufactured matzoh, the unleavened bread eaten during Passover.

Jews also craved seltzer, which could be consumed with a meal of meat without violating the kosher laws prohibiting the mixing of meat and dairy products. *Belchwasser* was made by more than a hundred firms in New York City in 1907. By horse and wagon, businesses delivered the universal refreshment to homes in the Jewish neighborhoods. Seltzermen, who hauled fifty-pound cases of the blue-and-green-glass siphon bottles of "workers' champagne," were beloved tradesmen.

The humorist Harry Golden, who grew up in a cold-water tenement on the Lower East Side, recalls the obsession with seltzer in the "Ate Congressional District." Every corner had a soda-water stand that sold seltzer and soda drinks made from the jars of cherry, raspberry, mulberry, and other preserves on the marble counter. If you wanted a glass of seltzer without syrup, your order was "Give me a small plain." For a large bubbly glass, you asked, "Give me for two cents plain."

"A comely young woman is eating her dinner of dry bread and green pickles," the reporter Jacob Riis wrote in his portrait of the Lower East Side. In the shtetls of Poland, Lithuania, Ukraine, and Russia, Jews developed an affection for pickled cabbage, beets, and cucumbers. The "sours," which fermented in cellars and outhouses, were preserved for winter dinners, their salty acidity an antidote to a starchy diet of black bread and potatoes. "Good food . . . should be accented with highly flavored relishes and pickles, including cucumbers, peppers, green tomatoes, and apples," anthropologists Mary Zborowski and Elizabeth Herzog remarked of the tastes of eastern European Jews.

Merchants in the new land followed in the footsteps of central European Jewish women who peddled pickles in village markets. Pickle dealers on the Lower East Side shouted "a nickel a shtickel." Sol Kaplan, a pickle dealer in the neighborhood, recalls the heyday of his product: "That time, every corner had a pickle store. People ate. It was European people. Americans don't eat that stuff much." Kaplan takes pride in the traditional techniques the sellers used:

After he buys 'em, then he'd throw 'em into barrels, make brine up, put in garlic and spice, water 'em and cover 'em up, press 'em down, that's all. The brine is made from salt and water. Then you put the spice in. . . . They didn't use mixed spices like we do now. They used to buy mostly cloves, the *nagelach*, and they bought hot peppers, and they use all kinds of coriander. It takes longer, but if you wanna make something good, you gotta do a lot of work. That's what the people came for.

A great deal of Jewish life revolved around fish. Herring, a mainstay in the diet of the poor European, also fed the American greenhorn. Prepared in sundry ways—pickled, fried, grilled, chopped—it could be served hot or cold. Garment workers wrapped herring, pickles, and black bread in newspaper for their lunch. In their adopted land of plenty, fish became a mark of economic advancement. The immigrant on the rise could afford lox, a luxury in the old world, instead of the common herring.

An emblem of fertility in the Jewish faith, fish symbolized the coming of the messiah. It was the centerpiece of the Sabbath dinner. For the Jewish housewife, forgetting the fish, the Jewish writer Sholom Aleichem quipped, is "worse than dying, for if she died it would be over and done with. But if she comes home without fish for the Sabbath, then she has to face her husband's anger. And that's worse than death."

Shopping for the Sabbath fish was a ritual for Jewish women, and they scrutinized closely the fish offered at the Hester Street market: "Big fish and little fish, light and dark fish, blue fish and white fish, fresh fish and not quite so fresh. . . . These people love fish and that fish is generally the piece de resistance of a Friday evening meal," the *New York Times* reported in 1894. "Shabbas fish, guefilte fish, fish cooked sweet and sour, indeed fish cooked and prepared in all the ways imaginable and in some ways quite beyond the realm of the ordinary imagination. . . . The fish is good kosher (clean) food and a particularly appropriate viand with which to usher in the Sabbath."

Denizens of the Lower East Side like Mollie Hyman relished memories of the fish merchants: "I had herring every day, once herring, once tomato herring, once sardines. Every grocery sold herring. You came in and you asked for a little herring. It would be three cents. He would give you a little herring. If you asked for a large herring, he would charge you six cents, but it was the same little herring."

Early Jewish businesses capitalized on these tastes. Joel Russ, a Galician who fled to America to escape service in the army, got his start peddling dried mushrooms, an eastern European fancy, first by horse and wagon and then from a pushcart on the Lower East Side. Russ, who had learned some of the tricks of the herring trade from his sister, opened his own shop, Russ's Cut-Rate Appetizers, on Orchard Street. Barrels of schmaltz (fatty) herring, lox, and pickles were his attractions. Beginning with a few basic products, this early "appetizing store" gradually increased its wares. Dried fruits and nuts, halvah, bagels, bialys, olives, and other tempting items filled up the shop.

Like Zabar's, the New York City emporium that also started as a purveyor of appetizers, the shop, now called Russ and Daughters, has evolved into a gourmet specialty business. Although basic lox and herring are still its calling cards, Russ and Daughters also is a purveyor of more sophisticated fare—Scottish salmon, gravlax, caviars, herring in mustard dill sauce, and a wide assortment of other fish; tofu cream cheese; and inventive salads and desserts.

The appetizing store was a New York City phenomenon. In 1936 thirty-six such shops were selling their wares in New York City. "Although people of every nationality patronize the retail appetizing stores, the Jewish people are by far the greatest customers," commented a researcher for the New Deal WPA program. "This may be attributed to their peculiar love for highly seasoned foods."

Bakeries abounded on the Lower East Side. They churned out breads and rolls—pumpernickel, black bread, rye, kaiser, *pletzls*, bialys—pastries, and cakes. The Sabbath dinner was incomplete without the challah, the beautifully braided loaf. Eastern European immigrants were especially nostalgic for the knish, the festive snack of their homelands. The rectangular pastry shell traditionally stuffed with a potato-and-onion filling developed into an everyday street food in America.

Yonah Schimmel, a small bakery located on Houston Street on the Lower East Side, was a fountainhead of the knish. The unadorned shop, a shrine today for Jewish visitors, was opened in 1910 by Mr. Schimmel, who had been a rabbi in eastern Europe. Schimmel, pictured with a black beard and skullcap in the store window, had first found work teaching Hebrew school. The pay was poor, and the new immigrant chose another, higher-paying vocation: baking knishes and selling them from a pushcart.

Schimmel, who also helped out as *shamis*, the sexton, of a nearby Romanian synagogue, decided to open his own shop. His knishes, filled with pot cheese, kasha, and other new fillings, emerged from the oven bigger and bulkier than their European cousins. They were sent by dumbwaiter from the basement kitchen to be noshed on in a small dining room of Formica tables or taken out. The eatery also prepared clabbered milk, whose sour flavor appealed to Schimmel's eastern European customers.

The shop attracted the common citizen and the affluent. "On Sunday rich people, very rich people, used to come in their cars and they would wait in line for hours," waiter Izzy Finklestein remembers. Politicians seized on the knish as a campaign prop. Candidates running in New York were photographed in newspapers savoring the pastry. Eleanor Roosevelt made a special stop at Schimmel's to buy a bag of knishes for her husband when he was campaigning in the district.

☆ ☆

Ethnic restaurants that combined eastern European dishes with a Jewish flavor burgeoned on the Lower East Side. Fancy dining rooms like Moskowitz and Lupowitz prepared old-world entrées such as Romanian skirt steak and serenaded the guests with gypsy violins. Bottles of seltzer greeted customers at their tables.

A less elegant institution, the dairy restaurant, gained a wide following in the urban shtetl. Two immigrants, Jacob and Herman Hormatz, were pioneers in a business invented in America. With a $150 stake, they opened a tiny eatery with eight oilcloth-covered tables on Pitt Street in the Lower East Side. Coffee cost three cents a cup and a meal twenty-five cents at the Harmatz Dairy Restaurant in 1905.

The climate was ripe for a dairy venture. Poor sanitation made residents fearful of meat, and even restaurants could not be trusted to keep it from spoiling. An epidemic of stomach illness in the neighborhood accentuated these fears.

The dairy restaurant's appeal was that it was clean, safe, and healthful. Moreover, it encouraged those who observed kosher to eat wholesome food that conformed with the dietary laws.

From the raw materials of eggs, fish, vegetables and fruits, grains, and dairy products, the Harmatzes fashioned an inventive "vegetarian dairy" cuisine. They started out with soups, whitefish, and other bland eastern European dishes but soon began enticing their customers with zestier food, with more vegetables and salads. The Harmatzes made eating dairy a sensual and pleasurable experience, not a religiously imposed hardship.

The original Pitt Street business begat two larger restaurants named Ratner's, one on Second Avenue in the East Village and the other on Delancey Street on the Lower East Side near the Williamsburg bridge. Their cooks reached into central European and Jewish cooking traditions to develop a repertoire of delicious soups, salads, and egg, fish, and dairy dishes.

Hearty, bracing soups were a Ratner's specialty. Customers lusted after the steaming or cold beet borscht, a soup that crossed all boundaries in eastern Europe, served with a potato or a dollop of sour cream. Customers sat down to eastern European favorites like mushroom barley. Carrots, celery, green peppers, lima beans, and onions baked in clarified butter made an exhilarating broth. The dried mushrooms were a traditional food in Poland, Lithuania, and the Ukraine. Diners nibbled onion rolls and chewed on rye, pumpernickel, raisin pumpernickel, and other crunchy breads while enjoying the robust fare.

Doughy delicacies pulled ravenous diners to Ratner's. Pocket pastries—blintzes and *pirogen*—were kin to the knish. The blintz, a Yiddish word derived from the Ukrainian *bliniscki* by way of the Russian word for pancakes, *blini,* was a crepe folded over any one of a variety of seductive fillings. The crispy blintz might be filled with cottage or farmer cheese. Some bulged with fruit—strawberries, blueberries, and apples. The pastry was blanketed with sour cream. *Pirogen,* a boiled or fried dumplinglike dish common in Russia and Poland, was stuffed with farmer cheese, cabbage, kasha, or fruit. Sour cream was again a standard accompaniment.

Kasha *varniskes,* a quintessential dairy plate, marries a basic peasant staple with another doughy food, bowtie noodles. Kasha, nutty-tasting buckwheat groats, was eaten as a porridge by Russians and Poles for breakfast and bulked up other meals of the day. In the Ratner's classic, onions are sautéed in oil or schmaltz until they are burned. The *varniskes,* Yiddish for the noodles, are boiled and then melded with the onions and kasha.

Fish was prominent in starter and main courses. Guests whetted their appetite with pickled herring, chopped herring, pickled lox, and chopped salmon, then fortified themselves with dinners of baked halibut, flounder, whitefish, and fried carp. Egg dishes were accented with the salty tang of fish; a menu favorite was scrambled eggs and smoked salmon.

Ratner's and other dairy restaurants concocted intriguing meat substitutes. Vegetable cutlets were made from patties containing a blend of mushrooms, carrots, green peas, eggs, and matzoh meal. Chopped liver, another Ratner's vegetarian specialty, was a regular item on dairy menus. The writer Isaac Singer enjoyed the dish, typically prepared from eggplant, lentils, or string beans, once a week at the Famous Dairy Restaurant on New York's Upper West Side.

Ratner's also showered its patrons with rich desserts. Danishes, strudel, noodle pudding, *rugelach,* and a plethora of other sweets were baked in its ovens. The recipes had the flavor of eastern Europe but the abundant display was exuberantly American.

The restaurant operated in the midst of a vibrant world of immigrant culture and entertainment. The Second Avenue restaurant was located in the Yiddish Rialto, or Knish Alley, a district that in its heyday boasted fifteen Yiddish theaters. Music stores carried Yiddish recordings, and the newsstands sold Yiddish newspapers. The Ratner's on Delancey Restaurant also thrived on the theatrical spirit of the Lower East Side. The Loews Delancey, a vaudeville house only a few steps away, frequently hosted performers such as Al Jolson, Fanny Brice, and the Ritz Brothers.

Cafés also became centers of Jewish cooking and companionship. The Garden Cafeteria, next door to the *Jewish Forward* newspaper, was a gathering place for reporters, actors, intellectuals, and ethnics who worked in the neighborhood. Like an eastern Europe café, it buzzed with conversation and animated debate. Places like the Garden encouraged a breed of ethnic socializers that Isaac Singer, who was one of them, dubbed "cafeterianiks."

The Garden, which opened in 1931, was organized like a cafeteria. Customers decided on their order, and the counterman punched the appropriate code on their ticket. There were the classic dairy choices—blintzes, *varniskes,* soups. The display case revealed tantalizing plates of smoked whitefish, herring and apple and other salads, cheese, and coffee cakes. Many diners were content with a piece of cake and tea or a bowl of chopped vegetables and fruit mixed with sour cream.

As the Lower East Side rag trade withered away, Jewish cafeterias and luncheonettes sprang up in the midtown garment center. Dubrow's, one of the most famous cafeterias, served up *pirogen,* gefilte fish, and roast chicken to cutters, jobbers, and pressmen. Irving Moskowitz, a Dubrow's cafeteria customer for over thirty years, remembered it as a warm gathering place: "It was more than just a place to eat. It was a meeting place. A place. You didn't get to know them [other customers]. But they were people, and you sort of knew them."

☆ ☆

Salami hung from hooks in the window, and from the wall of Katz's, the boisterous Lower East Side delicatessen. Overflowing with spicy and smoked meats, the eatery, founded in 1898, exemplified the early Jewish deli, which stood on the other side of the culinary divide from the dairy restaurant.

The Houston Street restaurant was crowded with customers who had their orders punched and proceeded down the cafeteria line, past the city's longest deli counter. They hungered for hot dogs drenched in sauerkraut, salami, pastrami, corned beef, and tongue. Knobblewurst, a garlicky frankfurter, was a customer favorite. Meat was so omnipresent that even omelettes were filled with tongue or salami.

Katz's rye-bread sandwiches were served with trimmings that latter-day delicatessen eaters would take for granted. There were cups of sharp mustard, bowls of pickles and sour tomatoes, and sides of french fries. Katz's made Heinz kosher baked beans another deli accessory. When the deli added table service, customers were treated to Jewish waiters' sardonic, smart-alecky humor. Writer Israel Shenker called them "the high priests of chutzpah."

The heaviness and the briny spiciness of the deli meal was often washed away with a tart glass of Dr. Brown's Cel-Ray tonic or the company's cream and black cherry sodas. Cel-Ray, the quintessential deli drink, was supposedly the brainchild of a Lower East Side physician. Dr. Brown, the legend goes, devised a tonic infused with celery seeds, seltzer, and sugar for sick children in the neighborhood. Deli aficionados were distinguished from amateurs by their familiarity with the beverage in the trademark green bottle. "Generation after generation was weaned on this stuff," observed Harry Gold, the company's marketing director.

Katz's achieved celebrity status in the 1940s with a sign placed in its window beseeching patrons to "Send a Salami to Your Boy in the Army." In a patriotic gesture, Katz shipped salamis to servicemen all over the world.

Still operating, the culinary temple is a must-see stop for visitors trying to recapture the ethnic past. Like so many other of the neighborhood's businesses, Katz's has been a magnet for politicians. Campaigning for the presidency, Al Gore met there in 2000 with Russian Prime Minister Victor Chernomyrdin for a "Deli Summit."

Jewish entrepreneurs transformed the delicatessen, an institution that German immigrants brought to America. In fact, "delicatessen" was their word for seller of "delicacies." The first of these stores had a strong German accent, L. H. Robins noted in the *New York Times*: "Their eats were confined to various kinds of kuchen, kraut, kase, fisch, brot, und so weiter. . . . When you opened the door a bell tinkled somewhere in the room and someone who said 'Ja' came forward to wait on you." The new proprietors replaced German specialties with meats prepared in an eastern European Jewish style and in accordance with the dietary laws.

The products in early shops reflected the national origins of different groups in the Jewish diaspora. "On Rivingston Street and on Allen Street, the Rumanian deli store was making its appearance with its goose pastrama and kegs of ripe olives and tubs of salted vine leaves," reminisced author M. E. Ravage.

The delicatessens gradually grew more uniform, becoming largely purveyors of pickled, cured, and smoked meats, which were too time-consuming to prepare at home. By the mid-1930s, 5,000 delis were serving customers in New York City. Brisket was cured in salt and seasoned with garlic, bay leaves, and black pepper for corned beef; tongue was pickled with similar seasonings. Frankfurters and salami were made with beef instead of pork and seasoned with spices. For customers who liked their hot dogs plump, the delis gave them "specials."

Pastrami, one of the most beloved deli meats, traveled to America along a long and intricate path. The Ottoman Turks learned about cured beef, writer John Ash suggests, from the Byzantines, whose empire they conquered. They called the meat *basturma*. It was a wind-dried beef, rubbed with cumin and red pepper and accented with garlic, and was usually sliced very thin.

The well-preserved meat was carried by the Turkish army on its military campaigns. Jewish peddlers in Romania, part of the Ottoman empire, learned the curing technique from the soldiers. The peddlers, food writer Joan Nathan points out, appropriated the product, made it kosher, and added more garlic, black pepper, and paprika.

Romanian Jewish immigrants introduced pastrami to America. Deli masters tinkered with the traditional recipe and created a moist, garlicky brisket that had been marinated in spices, smoked, and finally steamed.

Much more than an eatery, the delicatessen was becoming part of America's ethnic folkways. The immigrants took joy in the warmth and connection this urban refuge offered and delighted in its culinary rituals. The sensory experience of the delicatessen became part of the Jewish memory. In his memoir of growing up in Brownsville, an ethnic neighborhood in Brooklyn, Alfred Kazin writes lyrically of the pull of the delicatessen: "At Saturday twilight, as soon as the delicatessen store reopened after the Sabbath rest, we raced into it panting for the hot dogs sizzling on the gas plate just inside the window. The look of that blackened empty gas plate had driven us wild through the wearisome Sabbath day. And now, as the electric sign blazed up again, lighting up the words Jewish National Delicatessen, it was as if we had entered into our rightful heritage."

"Hot Dogs Mit Knishes": Jewish Food Comes to Main Street

Crowds flocked to the "spiritual home of the U.S. hot dog" in Coney Island in the early decades of the twentieth century. Nathan Handwerker, the Polish immigrant who founded this famed restaurant, along with a succession of other merchants, developed a mass market for Jewish food.

The first stirrings of hot-dog entrepreneurship began in late-nineteenth-century Coney Island, then a Brooklyn high-society resort of hotels and restaurants near the ocean. Clams were the popular food of the day. Vacationers dined on clam chowder, grilled clams, and other dishes.

Charles Feltman, a German-born pie vendor, pushed his cart along the beaches and trails of the resort. Feltman, who arrived in the

United States as a teenager and worked as a butcher, catered to the customers of the inns and the German lager-beer taverns. He began losing trade to the hotels when they started making hot dishes, and to regain his advantage, the pie man changed products. Since his wagon was too small to make hot sandwiches or to hold much cooking equipment, Feltman decided to sell hot sausages, for which his hometown of Frankfurt was famous.

He enlisted Donovan (only his first name is recorded), the wheelwright who had built his wagon, to convert it to frankfurter cooking. The mechanic installed a charcoal stove on top of which Feltman would boil the wieners in a kettle. Donovan also constructed a tin-lined chest to store the rolls and keep them fresh. From his wagon, Feltman now hawked "Frankfurter sandwiches" doused with mustard and sauerkraut. The hot dog was sold in a bun, a German custom. The milk rolls were warmed, an innovation of Feltman's.

After selling nearly 4,000 pork sausages in his first year, the hot-dog vendor's business boomed. Feltman invested his profits in a shore lot on which he built the Ocean Pavilion Hotel in 1874. He created a German-style entertainment center on the hotel property, complete with beer gardens, restaurants, and rollicking German bands. Throughout the complex, workers cooked hot dogs on seven large grills.

One summer day in 1915, a young Jewish immigrant saw a help-wanted sign on Feltman's restaurant. Nathan Handwerker, the son of a Polish shoemaker, started learning the craft from his father at the age of six. Handwerker, whose name means "day laborer," left his homeland for Belgium at age eighteen to find work in his trade. He worked just long enough to pay for his passage to America and shipped out in a converted cattle boat, arriving in New York in 1910 after a twenty-two-day voyage. Now twenty, Handwerker found a job at Max's Busy Bee, a Manhattan restaurant, where he washed dishes and worked the counter.

Handwerker applied for the job at Feltman's and was hired to deliver franks and slice rolls. He earned $11 a week, slept on the kitchen floor, and survived on free hot dogs. Handwerker dreamed of going into business for himself and of competing with Feltman's. When Feltman raised his hot-dog price to ten cents, two of his regulars, Eddie Cantor and Jimmy Durante, who performed at local clubs, encouraged Handwerker to offer a cheaper product. Durante and Cantor, who depended on Feltman's for their meals, cajoled their friend, "Open your place and sell the frankfurters at a price we can afford."

With $300 in capital, Handwerker put up a fifteen-foot stand on Surf Avenue across the street from Feltman's and started selling nickel hot dogs. Nathan's hot dogs were distinctive. In keeping with Jewish tradition, the griddle-cooked franks, unlike Feltman's, were all beef instead of pork. They were served up in toasted rolls, a novelty at the time. Nathan jumped into the competitive fray with a simple motto: "Give 'em and let 'em eat."

The stand originally had only an oilcloth sign that said "Hot Dogs." Nathan wanted to call it "Handwerker's Hot Dogs," but the name was too long for the sign. At that time, Sophie Tucker, a Coney Island saloon singer known as the "Red Hot Mama," was belting out a new tune, "Nathan, Nathan, Why You Waitin'?" Customers told Handwerker, "Hey, Nathan, you're getting famous. We keep hearing your name sung in that song all the time," son Murray recounted. His father then named the business Nathan's Famous.

To win customers, Nathan had to overcome the resistance of snobbish resort-goers who disdained the interloper's cut-rate franks. He came up with a gimmick, recruiting a group of medical interns to come to his stand dressed in white coats. "Be sure to have them come with stethoscopes dangling from their jackets," Nathan urged a friend, whose son was one of the interns. A sign went up at the shop: "If doctors eat hot dogs, you know they're good."

As the business gradually won acceptance, Nathan struggled to improve his product. One day he met Ida Greenwald, who worked at a soft-drink stand, and hired her to toast hot-dog rolls. Ida, whom Nathan would marry, developed a spicy recipe that imparted a garlicky zip to the juicy frankfurters.

Food and show business intersected at Nathan's. Handwerker hired Clara Boutinelli, a photogenic teenager, as a helper. She caught the eye of a movie talent scout. Boutinelli, who changed her name to Clara Bow, attained stardom as the It Girl in silent movies. Other aspiring entertainers like Jimmy Durante, Eddie Cantor, and Irving Berlin, all Coney Island singing waiters, became steady customers.

The social barriers to a Coney Island holiday crumbled when the New York City subway line finally reached the resort in 1920. Ordinary city dwellers could now leave their tenements behind and take a day trip to Coney Island for the price of a nickel. The building of the boardwalk in 1923 lured a multitude of new customers to Nathan's. The restaurant was located on a direct path between the subway station and the boardwalk. If Feltman's represented an older, tradition-bound era, Nathan's rode the democratic wave of popular entertainment.

Nathan was popularizing an affordable, portable snack when a sit-down meal was beyond the reach of many. A mecca for the urban immigrant, the eatery was especially cherished by Jewish ethnics. Yiddish entertainers, historian Jenna Joselit points out, sang its praises. In 1926 singer Molly Picon raved: "At Coney Island you can buy a delicatessen red hot to eat as you walk along the boardwalk." A year later Aaron Lebdoff carried on the celebration with his song "Hot Dog Mit Knishes."

Nathan's quickly outgrew its space and mushroomed into a block-long eatery. Like his entertainer patrons, Handwerker was a shameless promoter. He plastered his eatery with green-and-white signs that "shrieked like fire engine sirens," as writer Edo McCullough put it. A host of come-ons filled the placards: "Stop here—this is the only original New York frankfurter of Coney Island," "All Our Food Fresh Daily," and "Original Nathan's Famous Frankfurters."

Like carnival barkers, the countermen yelled and shouted, pitching products to the throngs. Handwerker himself greeted customers and glad-handed visiting celebrities. Behind the twenty-foot counter, cashiers tallied up the charges. The business sold its millionth hot dog on July 6, 1955.

Politicians latched onto the frankfurter. At his home in Hyde Park, F.D.R. served a Nathan's hot dog to a surprised King George of England. A stop at Nathan's became a campaign ritual. In 1958, Nelson Rockefeller paid homage to the eatery while campaigning for governor of New York. Photographed while eating a hot dog, he told the press: "No man can hope to get elected in New York State without being photographed eating hot dogs at Nathan's Famous."

Nathan's ethnic identity blurred over the years. New generations who traveled to Coney Island were unaware of the business's Jewish immigrant roots. While concentrating on the hot dog, the emporium diversified. It marketed corn on the cob, french fries, and beer. Handwerker added oysters and clams, distinctly nonkosher items, to the menu to appeal to an even wider group of customers.

☆ ☆

The delicatessen too was reaching a broader audience. The shops, which were turning into full-fledged restaurants, were no longer isolated in Jewish enclaves. They were moving to Main Street.

Reuben's and Lindy's, two of the pioneering New York City delicatessens, were infused with the glamour and electricity of Broadway. Arnold Reuben had a "Broadway nervous tempo manner," an interviewer observed, with intonations that were "mixed Yiddish, Broadway wise guy . . . and big man." The one-time peddler opened what he called "a little shtoonky delicatessen store" on Broadway in 1915. He expanded into the restaurant business in the 1920s. Reuben's became famous for triple-decker rye sandwiches, an ethnic variation on the American club sandwich. Reuben named his creations for entertainers like Al Jolson, Eddie Cantor, and other celebrities, who frequented his establishment.

The restaurant's trademark sandwich was named after the proprietor. There are many legends about the origin of the Reuben. "Our German chef in 1929 . . . made it for me because I only ate hamburgers while I was running the restaurant," Mr. Reuben recounted. "It was

corned beef, toasted on very black Russian pumpernickel, with sauerkraut and imported melted Swiss cheese." Whether or not he was its
originator, the restaurateur made the sandwich a standard of the deli
repertoire. "From a sandwich to an institution," the Reuben's slogan
went.

Leo Lindemann, a German immigrant, who apprenticed in a
Berlin delicatessen as a young boy, put himself through a crash course
in the American restaurant business. He trained to be a waiter at the
Hotel Marie Antoinette in New York City and took a series of jobs
waiting tables. The go-getter became a headwaiter at Gertners restaurant in Times Square and in 1921, eight years after coming to America, launched his own Broadway restaurant.

A late-night haunt of comedy writers, entertainers, and gangsters,
Lindy's was immortalized as "Mindy's" by the writer Damon Runyon.
Customers enjoyed the antics of Al Jolson and Harpo Marx.
"Through this maze of nonsense moved Lindy, hands folded on his
stomach, darting this way and that," columnist Robert Sylvester observed. The theater-district restaurant was the birthplace of inventive
sandwiches. Lindy dreamed up smoked turkey and chicken liver, sturgeon and nova, and other combinations. The impresario sent salami,
herring, cheesecake, and other samples of his wares to his friends in
the White House and the political world.

New York City's Carnegie Delicatessen carried on the legacy of
Lindy's and Reuben's. Founded in 1935 as a butcher shop, the midtown restaurant offers a mammoth menu of appetizers, soups, salads,
sandwiches, and entrées that bridges the divide between dairy and
delicatessen. Customers can choose between gargantuan corned beef
and pastrami sandwiches, triple-deckers like "Tongues for the Memory" (tongue, corned beef, and Swiss with coleslaw and Russian
dressing), blintzes, *pirogen*, pickled herring, and potato pancakes.
This clubhouse for wise-cracking comedians like Jackie Mason and
Henny Youngman, celebrated in Woody Allen's movie *Broadway
Danny Rose*, also serves up full-scale dinners of brisket, Hungarian
goulash, and Romanian chicken paprikash. When delicatessens like

the Carnegie served hot roast beef and turkey sandwiches with coleslaw and french fries, it was more proof the deli had lost its alien edge.

Vita and Breakstone: Jewish Food in the Supermarket

It was not only restaurateurs who were popularizing Jewish food. Wholesalers, manufacturers, and food processors also played a critical role. Isaac Breakstone, a dairy merchant, was one such businessman.

Breakstone, born Breghstein, grew up on the family farm above the Lithuanian village of Ponieman, which was located on a high plateau above the river Nieman. In this shtetl, the Breghsteins lived a simple economical life, butchering their own meat, dairying, and growing their own produce. They ate basic meals of potatoes, sour milk, pickles, and bread.

The villages of eastern Europe, food historian Claudia Roden points out, supported a lively dairy business. The butter, sour cream, buttermilk, and cream cheese the Jews made were put in large earthenware pots or wrapped in leaves and traded in open-air markets. Milkmen delivered fresh milk from the farms daily to their customers.

To escape conscription in the czar's army, Isaac Breghstein left Ponieman for America in 1882, arriving in New York City at age fifteen. After a period of peddling, first encyclopedias and then milk, Isaac and his brother, Joseph, who had emigrated earlier, decided to start a small dairy business. "It was the only thing they knew," his grandson, Sanford Claster, observed. They wholesaled butter, cottage or farmer cheese, and sour cream to stores that catered to the Jewish community.

Eastern European Jews wanted the familiar "fresh, white cheeses that were considered kosher, having barely emerged from their incarnation as cream," writer Ruth Gay observes. Several kinds of cheese met the test, she continues. "Molded into loaves, they were called farmer cheese. Pressed through a fine sieve and with a little added cream, the product was cottage cheese; pressed through a coarser sieve and left to dry, it was pot cheese." Isaac himself, "a strong silent type," grandson Stanley Leavy remembers, enjoyed a breakfast dish of pot cheese, sour cream, and scallions.

"They had a natural area to feed," Sanford Claster observed. The partners hired jobbers to sell their product to small groceries and dairy stores. The salesmen "spread out all over New York City," Claster said. In the 1920s the Breakstones contracted with upstate New York dairy farmers to supply their business. A plant in Downsville, New York, started mass producing their signature cream cheese, which would overtake farmer cheese and pot cheese in popularity.

The brand gained a following. Loyal buyers grew attached to the small trucks with the company name that drove through the city. Shoppers cherished the containers Breakstone's supplied to retailers at a time when the cheese was marketed in bulk. Isaac Breakstone "would come home from the office with bottles of sour cream and the wonderful wooden boxes of cream cheese with the family name proudly printed in a flowing script," Stanley Leavy recalls.

From the beginning, the Breakstones wanted to appeal to a larger market, to reach ethnic and nonethnic alike. Their early cottage cheese tins proclaimed the Americanness of the product. The figure of a be-wigged colonial Yankee graced the container.

Cream cheese, a homegrown item, was not a strange food to many Americans. It was already being manufactured as early as 1881 by a company in Chester, New York. Breakstone introduced cream cheese to an even wider audience when it opened plants in America's heart-land—Ladysmith, Wisconsin, and Freeport, Illinois.

Cream cheese also won the affection of Jewish consumers. They felt an affinity for dairy food that was similar to the fresh eastern Euro-pean cheeses of their heritage. Cream cheese soon was an essential part of the food habits of the immigrants in their new home. Putting a schmear of cream cheese, often Breakstone's, on a bagel became a culinary ritual. The custom crossed over to the mainstream, and cream cheese took its place as an essential accompaniment to the American brunch.

Cheesecake, another vital element in the dairy tradition, was also absorbed into the commercial mainstream. The dessert, inherited from eastern Europe, was steeped in religious tradition. It is typically eaten during the Shavuot festival, which honors the revelation of the Torah on Mt. Sinai and also celebrates the spring harvest. Cheesecake was a fitting dessert for a holiday that marked the gift of "milk and honey."

American cheesecake became the crown jewel of the Jewish restaurant. It could cap a dairy meal or climax a meaty lunch in a kosher-style deli. Lindy's and Reuben's showcased the dessert. Each restaurant proclaimed its cheesecake the "original." Reuben's cheesecake, Arnold Reuben Jr. recalls, was unique because it was baked with cream cheese. "Everybody else was making it with cottage cheese in those days." Lindy's adorned its cakes with strawberries and other fruits, a flourish unknown in the old country. The eastern European sweet soon became known as "New York cheesecake."

A Jewish baker in Chicago took cheesecake into the supermarket. Charles W. Lubin, who had learned the baking trade at age fourteen in Decatur, Illinois, a Chicago suburb, liked to experiment with dessert ideas. With $1,500, he and his brother-in-law bought a chain of neighborhood bakeries, which they named Community Bake Shops. In 1949, Lubin created a "cream cheese cake" that he called Sara Lee after his eight-year-old daughter. "Sara Lee sounds wholesome and American somehow," the baker recalls.

Not content with over-the-counter sales, Lubin wanted to break into the chains. Supermarkets and restaurants snapped up his cheesecake. The business grew, moving to even larger facilities and building its own plant. Renamed the Kitchens of Sara Lee, Lubin's company was now baking pecan all-butter coffee cake and all-butter pound cake in addition to its trademark cheesecake.

Lubin, a believer in national distribution, searched for a technique to realize his vision. When a buyer from Texas in 1952 asked for a shipment of cakes, he found a solution. Lubin developed an aluminum foil baking pan in which to bake his products and froze the cakes in the same container in which they would later be sold in the supermarket. The desserts could now be manufactured and distributed from a central plant, all the while retaining their freshness.

In 1954, Sara Lee's cakes were being marketed in forty-eight states. Attractive products and an ingenious production and distribution system excited larger companies in the small enterprise. Consolidated Foods Corporation acquired the business in 1956, and the Kitchens of Sara Lee became a subsidiary of the corporation with Charles Lubin as CEO.

☆ ☆

Even the knish could not escape mass production. Elias Gabay, a shoemaker from the former Yugoslavia, left his homeland for New York in 1919. Arriving with thirty-five cents in his pocket, he found work in shoe factories. Because he was frequently unemployed, Gabay decided to go into business for himself. He and his wife, Bella, started a small basement restaurant on the Lower East Side. One day a customer ordered blintzes with potatoes instead of cheese. Bella prepared the item, which was a reasonable facsimile of a knish. The product was a hit, and the couple, who had been married in a Yugoslav town named Nish, concentrated on making knishes.

Elias hawked the knishes from a pushcart on the Lower East Side and on Coney Island. Increasing demand spurred the "King of Potato Pies" to invent machinery to mass produce his pastries. "We wanted to get away from hand labor," grandson Elliott recalls. In a Williamsburg, Brooklyn, factory, Gabay built a "Rube Goldberg" contraption, as Elliott describes it. Writer Israel Shenker, who visited the plant in the 1960s, marveled at the production technique: "molds and pipes and transmission belts jostle for space and glory. An intricate complex of potato washer and sorter leads to steamer and masher and drainpipe. . . . A stainless steel horizontal hand moves rhythmically up and down, patting each *knish* . . . as it passes."

The invention gave the business an early lead, which it maintained. "We were the first to automate knishes," Elliott, who now runs the company, says of his grandfather's contribution. Smaller knish makers could supply only a tiny piece of the market. Gabila's, the name Elias gave the business because Gabay was difficult to pronounce, initially marketed to delicatessens. "In the beginning, there were no supermarkets," Elliott notes.

When the supermarkets became ascendant, Gabila's reaped its largest gains there. Packages of fresh pastries and, beginning in the 1990s, frozen knishes flew through the chains. Customers in New York, New Jersey, and the Connecticut area are the largest buyers of the products. Florida is next, "where there are a lot of people who moved out," Elliott says. "You don't find much happening in Wyoming."

In the 1960s, Gabila's began vending knishes in food carts in Times Square and other commercial areas in New York City. Baseball and football stadiums were another target. Sports sales have soared. At a typical football game at Giants Stadium today, Elliott says, fans will consume 5,000 to 8,000 knishes.

In addition to the original potato, Gabila's knishes today are manufactured in kasha, spinach, broccoli, mixed vegetable, and mushroom flavors. Shoppers can choose among large, junior, and knishette (cocktail party) sizes. For the weight-conscious, Gabila's sells a fat-free product.

The knish's appeal has spread far beyond its original ethnic following. It appears in the inventory that the Boar's Head Company sells to mainstream delis and specialty groceries throughout the country. Although the Gabila knish is kosher, the label does not hurt its popularity. It enhances it, says Elliott. "Kosher is a big entity in today's market. People respect the word kosher."

Non-Jews who were introduced to knishes while growing up have a hard time giving up the treat. "Hispanics carry boxes under their arms to Puerto Rico," Elliott says.

☆ ☆

Herring and smoked fish, those passions of the Jewish immigrant, would also find their way onto the supermarket counter and into the American kitchen. Two young Czech Jews, Victor and George Heller, who arrived in New York City in the early 1900s, were savvy merchandisers on this culinary frontier. These German-speaking immigrants found jobs in a delicatessen in Yorkville, a German section of the city.

Herring, a fish they loved from their childhood, was one of the shop's biggest sellers. It appealed to Jewish shoppers as well as to Poles, Germans, and other European immigrants. "In the old country, it was a staple food for them," Aaron Gilman, Victor Heller's son-in-law, observed. After gaining several years of retail experience, the two brothers opened their own delicatessen in 1915 and soon thereafter launched two more.

Herring was selling so briskly in their stores that the brothers decided to go into the packing business. Initially, they imported herring and put it up in kegs, baskets, and barrels in a building on Hudson Street in lower Manhattan. They divided up the responsibilities: George handled the packing side; Victor lined up customers.

They marketed an "institutional pack" to restaurants, delicatessens, and mom-and-pop stores. In fact, in the early days, they sold their product to "anyone who would buy it," Mr. Gilman, who became an executive with the business, commented. After trying cardboard containers, the Hellers began packing their herring in jars, their most radical marketing breakthrough. Before that shoppers "would pick them out of a barrel and wrap them in a newspaper," Mr. Gilman noted.

World War I slowed the herring business. Victor went into the army, and the business's imports from Europe stopped. George improvised by organizing a domestic herring fleet that sailed from Provincetown. Business rebounded in the 1920s, and the Hellers expanded into smoked fish, another popular ethnic item. They acquired an old-time smoking business, the Richard Schnibbe Company, and started processing salmon, whitefish, and sturgeon in its Brooklyn plant. Constantly looking for new product lines, the brothers added olives and caviar to their list.

In 1930 the Hellers formed the Vita Food Products Company, which merged their enterprise with a number of smaller operations they had purchased. Vita became their products' brand name as well; the name came from the bulk item they had been buying from the F. H. Phillips Company, a business in Lovenstoft, England, near the Scottish border. Vita, which meant "health" in Latin, also, they felt, had a nice ring to it.

The enterprise was still a modest one, however, and it was not until the 1950s and 1960s that sales rose. Vita, which grew into a $40–$50 million-a-year business, no longer had to depend on the small retailer. The supermarkets, which emerged as a marketing force after the war, bought an ever growing share of its products. The Hellers diversified, expanding into maraschino cherries, sweet and sour pickles, mushrooms, and red and green peppers. The company also acquired more businesses, bought fishing boats, and built modern plants, canneries, and smokehouses.

But herring was still the foundation of their company. Starting with bismarck, the small whole fish, Vita introduced herring fillets and then herring tidbits. After the war, the Hellers brought out their best-known product, herring in cream sauce. Vita herring was "one of the first convenience foods that people could buy," Aaron Gilman says. "They could take it home and consume it with a piece of black bread."

Advertising broadened the appeal of the product. An endearing character, the herring maven, began appearing in ads in the 1960s promoting the brand. "Get Vita at your favorite supermarket, grocery, or delicatessen. Tell them the beloved Maven sent you. It won't save you any money, but you'll get the best herring," a 1965 advertisement in the *Hadassah* newsletter told readers.

Vita moved from the ethnic press to the general media, to newspapers and television. One of their newspaper ads for herring tidbits showed an empty jar. The caption read, "Herring Maven Strikes Again." Maven, a Yiddish word, which came from the Hebrew for "understanding," was at that time not widely known outside of Jewish circles. In a clever strategy, Vita employed an ethnic expression for "expert" to give their herring cachet.

Vita has shed its immigrant past. Few except the company's oldest customers know the origins of its products. Now owned by an investment group based in Chicago, Vita sells its herring and nova standards as well as salmon spread, marinated salmon, salmon burgers, herring fillets in wine sauce, shrimp cocktail, salad dressings, and an array of other goods. "In the distant past, the Vita brand was known for its quality line of kosher products which were purchased by an ethnically narrow consumer base," a report on the company noted. "The market consisted primarily of Jewish adherents to religious dietary law. However, today, over three-quarters of Vita's product end users are non-Jewish." In modern merchandising language, Aaron Gilman sums up the progress of Vita herring: The Heller brothers transformed it from a "bulk, unbranded product to a packaged, branded product." From barrel to supermarket shelf—a change that would have amazed the peddlers of the Lower East Side.

CHAPTER 5

From Chow Mein to Singapore Noodle: Inventing Chinese Food

Gold Mountain Folks: Chinese Food on the Western Frontier

CONTAINERS STOCKED WITH ORANGES, dried oysters, mushrooms, dried bean curd, bamboo shoots, duck eggs, sausages, ginger, and other food-stuffs were arriving in San Francisco's Yerba Buena Cove in the 1850s. Boxes of chopsticks, chopping knives, ladles, lacquer ware, iron and copper pans, and other kitchen implements, historian Robert Spier discovered, were carried off ships from China. The city on the bay was the gateway for South China's immigrants to California, the Gold Mountain of their dreams, and the entry point for the goods on which they depended.

An early trickle of sailors, students attending Christian schools, and clerks working for merchants was followed by a flood of pioneers. Twenty thousand immigrants from South China disembarked in San Francisco in 1852. Most of the voyagers, who first traveled by ship or raft to the ports of Hong Kong or Canton, came from an inhospitable region close to the South China Sea. They had grown up in villages in the district of Toishan in southeastern Kwangtung province, which is cut off by mountains from the rest of China. Successive migrations of Toishanese would make them the largest group in America's Chinese diaspora. Since few Americans knew Toishan, they called themselves Cantonese.

The ancestors of the immigrants had left North China to settle in the territory, whose name meant "elevated mountain." Its people scratched out a living working rocky, hilly farms, fishing, and engaging in petty trade. The environment bred adventurers, who sought an escape route on the open seas.

Toishan was close to the ports of Canton, Hong Kong, and Macau, China's few trading centers with the West. By the early nineteenth century, California merchants had already begun trading sea otter skins and other products with the East. Seamen and missionaries told the Toishanese dazzling stories of their glorious country.

Their prospects in China grew bleaker because of floods, typhoons, overpopulation, and bitter poverty. When news of the 1848 gold strikes in California reached them, peasants already familiar with the fabled West Coast needed little push to set off for America.

The "passenger immigrants" borrowed from family or took loans from merchants, contractors, and ship captains to pay for their trip. They were expected to repay these debts with interest from their earnings. Although often denigrated as "coolies," the immigrants were bold and enterprising individuals determined to improve their own and their families' fortunes. They were usually single men who planned to return home after amassing sufficient savings.

When they sailed into San Francisco, merchants or representatives of the "Six Companies," the commercial houses to which many of the newcomers were tied by clan or homeland connections, greeted them and put them up in lodging houses. Their stay in *dai fou* (big city) was brief, only long enough to get outfitted and supplied for a trip to the "diggings." They trekked from San Francisco to San Jose or climbed on steamers that sailed from Yerba Buena Cove up the Sacramento and San Jose Rivers to the mining country.

The sight of the novice miners tramping from the river ports to their campsites intrigued one California observer. They wore blue knee-length tunics, baggy trousers, and "huge basket hats made of split bamboo," the writer J. D. Borthwick noted in 1856. The immigrants pitched tents and constructed brush houses along the rivers, creeks, and streams they were prospecting.

The placer miners were forced to pick through the leftovers, the claims the white miners had abandoned or shunned. In spite of their disadvantage, the Chinese were met with venomous resentment from their rivals. They were harassed, beaten, robbed, evicted from their camps, and killed. Pressure from the established prospectors led to a state law that charged the Chinese miner a $3.00 monthly tax. In spite of the xenophobic climate, the Chinese managed to build a beachhead on the California frontier. Eighty percent of the Chinese in California, where the majority of the immigrants had settled, stuck with mining throughout the 1850s and 1860s.

The Chinese clung to their traditional food habits and created ingenious networks to supply their needs. Merchant houses in San Francisco organized shipments of goods to the mining outposts. River steamers transported noodles, yams, and peanut oil as well as joss sticks (incense sticks burned in front of idols), brushes, ink, firecrackers, and other sentimental articles. Sacks, jars, bottles, and woven baskets holding these products were transferred to wagons or pack mules for the trip to the mining camps.

Small stores sprang up in Chinese enclaves to sell provisions to the miners. The import houses sent out representatives to stock the shops and to develop a clientele. The agents were the miners' links to their villages. They carried letters from their families, which the merchants would read to those unable to do so; the storekeepers also helped the miners craft letters in response. The immigrants exchanged their gold for coin at the stores, and import houses arranged the remittance of funds to their families.

A mining-camp store in Camanche, California, whose records were unearthed by historian Sucheng Chan, sold both staples and more exotic ingredients. A sack of imported rice was priced at $6.00, a basket of tea leaves at $13.25. The shop carried ginger, *cam chun* (dried lily stalks used in cooking), and a variety of medicinal herbs. Merchants also sold chicken, pork, and duck, which they bought from immigrant farmers and butchers.

The South Chinese were ardent vegetable eaters. Miners originally grew their own produce, but soon they were buying *choy*—cabbage, mustard greens, green beans, spring onions—from fellow immigrants who devoted themselves full-time to truck farming. Farmers in Marysville, a town in the Sacramento Valley where Chinese vegetables flourished, traveled a distance to reach their customers. They hauled their much-coveted bitter melon and string beans to the prospectors by horse and wagon.

☆ ☆

New opportunities beckoned to the Chinese pioneers. Mineral strikes in the Rocky Mountains in the 1860s and 1870s and massive hiring by the Central Pacific Railroad lured them to new areas of the West. As new colonies of miners and railway men emerged in Utah, Montana, Colorado, Idaho, and other states, merchants followed bringing food.

Ox teams loaded with rice imported from China hauled it from Helena, Montana, to the remote settlement of Blackfoot City, Idaho. Pack trains were the culinary lifeline of miners in Silver City, Idaho. Chinese cooks, who prepared the meals in all of the city's boardinghouses for miners, depended on the supplies.

Chinese labor was indispensable to the Western railroads. Charles Crocker, the Central Pacific construction chief, snared 10,000 laborers to complete his line's western leg. His boss, Leland Stanford, was impressed by the virtues of the workmen: "As a class they are quiet, peaceable, patient, industrious, and economical."

"Crocker's pets," as the Chinese were called, toiled at backbreaking tasks. "The rugged mountains looked like stupendous ant hills," a *New York Tribune* reporter wrote. "They swarmed with Celestials, shoveling, wheeling, carting, and drilling, and blasting rock and earth." Food purveyors set up shop along the railway lines. From improvised railcar stores they sold bowls, chopsticks, pipes, and lamps. A shop in Merced,

California, that catered to rail gangs in the 1870s provided them dried seaweed, dried bean sprouts, dried abalone, and other foods.

Organized in gangs of twelve to twenty men, each crew was supplied with its own cook. "Send up more cooks," Jack Strawbridge, the railroad's Irish work chief, exclaimed, as he struggled to keep his troops content and fed. Both the Rocky Mountain miners and railroad workers were sticklers for their own food. The Chinese scorned the fare of beans, bread, beef, potatoes, and contaminated water given the white miners. Cooks fashioned meals from shipments of dried oysters, dried shrimp, salted cabbages, bacon, crackers, candies, and rice. The gangs drank barrels of tea and brewed leaves, roots, and bark to make traditional remedies. White workers looked with disgust at the "un-Christian food."

Virulent attacks against the Chinese continued in these new locations. Homes were burned, immigrants lynched and raped, and miners expelled from their claims. Work soon dried up. When the Central Pacific line was completed, there were few opportunities to replace the lost jobs.

☆ ☆

[T]he scent of sandalwood and exotic herbs from the drug stores, the sickly sweetness of opium smoke, the fumes of incense and raw pork, and the pungent odors from the sausages and raw meat.

Arnold Genthe
Remembering San Francisco's Chinatown, 1936

Many of the dispossessed sought refuge in San Francisco's Chinatown. Once primarily a way station and provisioning post for immigrants embarking for the frontier, it was blossoming into a full-fledged ethnic quarter. The enclave provided lodging, jobs, cultural life, and, most important, security. "Here they breathe easier," Reverend Otis Graham wrote in 1877. "The hoodlum's voice has died in the distance. Here Chinese faces delight the vision and Chinese voices greet the ear."

In its infancy, in the mid-1850s, Chinatown was a tiny two-block section conveniently close to the wharves where the boats dropped new arrivals. The community of 3,000 was sprouting butcher shops, general stores, barbershops, pharmacies, and other businesses to serve its mix of permanent residents and of transients moving back and forth from their mining outposts. Merchant houses that imported goods from their homeland ruled the quarter. In one year, 1853, the powerhouses unloaded more than 400,000 bags of rice from China.

The few "Occidentals" who visited Chinatown in the early years gaped at the curious products. The stores were "stocked with hams, tea, dried fish, dried ducks, and other very nasty looking Chinese vegetables, besides copper pots and kettles, fans, shawls, chessmen, and all sorts of curiosities," the writer J. D. Borthwick remarked.

Chinatown's population burgeoned to more than 12,000 in 1870 and to 22,000 ten years later. By the early twentieth century, the quarter, the country's largest Chinese community, stretched to fifteen blocks. The streets had a lively and varied commercial life. Peddlers hawked "toys, peanuts, dried lichees, poultry, cigars, sweets, and Chinese narcissus," to the bachelors who lived in crowded tenements and lodging houses. Food shops sold a profusion of mystifying products. "In the butcher shops were fat tubs of cold, clammy rice for those who lacked kitchen facilities and in the bakeries cakes stuffed with rice or sesame seeds or bits of pork, or chopped hazelnuts," writer Charles Dobie observed.

The urban Chinese relied on produce stores for an unusual assortment of fruits and vegetables they had once grown themselves. Charles Dobie stared at "beans in sprouting condition, Chinese parsley, a turnip that is peculiarly Chinese shaped like a dirigible; the bark of a bush that is fried with pork until it is crisp. If you chance to see a basket of lily bulbs in a food shop do not imagine that they are for spring planting. They are to be eaten, after they have been chopped fine and fried."

Ti, the heroine of a novel by Mary Bamford set in San Francisco's Chinatown, was captivated by another display: "some yellow squares of bean curd were piled for sale. Each square of curd was marked with a Chinese character. . . . Long pieces of sugar cane, brought from China, stood up against the side of the building, like so many fishing poles or pieces of bamboo."

Although the Chinese labored in cigar, shoe, and woolen factories, the immigrants gravitated increasingly to jobs providing personal service. Shielded from the hostility of white workers who kept trying to drive them out of choice jobs, they assumed the domestic chores of cooking, cleaning, and gardening for city families. The stereotype of the dutiful Chinese servant took hold. "It is not true that the Chinese are filthy in their habits, inefficient in their work, or untrustworthy. As cooks, domestic servants, launderers, and for orchard and vegetable garden work they have no superior," historian H. H. Bancroft commented.

In the farming and mining country, the Chinese cook performed a multitude of tasks. On farms, he cooked dinners, ran the household, and often managed the homestead itself. The Chinese cook was so often taken for granted as to be invisible to his boss. A Miss Hillyer of Virginia City gradually recognized an unfamiliar face in her kitchen. "Why, you're not Charlie," she said. "Charlie he go two weeks. Charlie he go China," the new cook answered.

It was a short step from family or work-camp cooking to the restaurant business. San Francisco's Chinatown spawned a host of eateries, which became an important source of employment for the newcomers. Triangular flags of yellow silk announced restaurants with evocative names—"Fragrant Almond Chamber," "A Garden of the Golden Valley," "Chamber of the Odors of Different Lands."

Tsing Tsing Lee, a restaurateur in 1850s San Francisco, hatched the widely imitated "dollar house" formula. He hung a roast pig at the entrance to The Balcony of Golden Joy and Delight, his 400-seat establishment, to welcome diners. The drawing cards, borrowed from the mining-camp boarding house, were dollar meal tickets—twenty-one meals for twenty dollars. More than a thousand hens were tied to stakes in the restaurant's backyard to fill the many orders of boiled chicken and rice.

These restaurants were a step up from the early scruffy eateries. "They opened their first eating-houses at the end of Kearny Street: smoky lairs where the cooking was an infamy and the comestibles barely decent enough to mention," writer Idwal Jones reported. Basement canteens continued to offer the colony's bachelors beef porridge and other hearty soups, fish, wonton, and basic snacks.

Chinese restaurants were beginning to attract the "Occidental" trade. Gold miners laying over in San Francisco in 1851 discovered scrumptious plates at one ethnic house. Miner William Shaw praised the fare: "The best eating houses in San Francisco are those kept by Celestials and conducted Chinese fashion. The dishes are mostly curries, hashes, and fricassees, served upon small dishes as they are exceedingly palatable. I was not curious enough to enquire as to the ingredients."

But many customers were squeamish about the strange meals. Writer Benjamin Taylor was revolted by a "four bits" dinner of "pale cakes with a waxen look, full of meats . . . then more cakes full of seeds . . . then giblets of you know what." Chinese cooks keenly adapted. Cheap and filling meals of beef steak, rice, and potatoes pleased early Chinese restaurant patrons in San Francisco.

Kitchen hands in frontier towns had already learned to make the adjustment. Despite their reputation as "filthy cooks," the immigrants won a popular following dispensing plentiful Western food. Late-nineteenth-century Chinese restaurants in the mining region, often called "English kitchens" to conceal their ownership, served up roast beef, french toast, chocolate cake, and white bread. In Prescott, Arizona, which had a small Chinatown, immigrants took over saloon restaurants previously owned by whites on the town's rough-and-tumble "whiskey row." To attract workmen, the chophouses fed them steak, fried eggs, potatoes, and steaming coffee.

Chinese cooks demonstrated a flair for culinary ingenuity, for converting the paltriest ingredients into novel and appetizing dishes. Western folklore is replete with legends of meals created by frugal chefs, who had developed economical habits in the harsh conditions of their homeland.

The Western sandwich, story has it, was concocted by a cook for a railway or mining work gang who put a filling of eggs, onions, peppers, and ham, a variation on egg foo yung, between two pieces of toast. The legend of the "hangtown fry," a popular California treat, is based on another resourceful chef. In one version, a gold miner flush from a successful dig asked for the "most expensive dish in the house" at an eatery in Placerville, California. The cook scrambled eggs with onions and then folded oysters into them, inventing a kind of California egg foo yung.

The most famous Chinese food tales concern the invention of chop suey. Li Hung Chang, an envoy of the Chinese emperor, became infatuated with the dish during a visit to America in 1896. In various tellings, he enjoyed the dish either at a banquet or at a New York Chinatown restaurant; in either case, he relished a dinner that cooks whipped up from leftover bits of meat and vegetables.

Chop suey derives from *za sui*, a word used by the people of Toishan, the homeland of the bulk of the immigrants, that means "different pieces" or "miscellaneous scraps." The thrifty Chinese cooks typically prepared chop suey by cooking entrails and giblets with bean sprouts, celery, and other vegetables in either a stir-fry or soup.

Another story has chop suey being improvised by a Chinese cook for a group of ravenous gold miners. They arrived late in the evening at a San Francisco café demanding to be fed. Since there was little in the kitchen, the cook fried up scraps of meat and vegetables and called the mélange chop suey.

Restaurateurs capitalized on the Li Hung Chang story to give luster to chop suey, advertising it as the mandarin's favorite. Chop suey houses mushroomed in the fledgling Chinatowns. By 1902 and 1903, eateries featuring the novelty were luring customers in Philadelphia, Pittsburgh, Chicago, Boston, and other cities.

New York City boasted three to four hundred chop suey houses in the 1920s. "All New York gleams at night with chop suey restaurants," English journalist Stephen Graham wrote in 1927. The crowd pleaser was replacing the traditional "chow chop suey," a stew of chicken livers and gizzards, fungi, bamboo buds, tripe, and bean sprouts.

The new version was more pleasing to the American palate. Chicken, beef, or pork was substituted for the repugnant tripe and giblets. Chop suey was made into a sanitized hash that could encompass a hodgepodge of items. A diner in turn-of-the-century New York dug into a "mess of veal, mushrooms, parsley, and a kind of macaroni with a peculiar pungent sauce."

The boom in chop suey strengthened the restaurant niche that the immigrants were carving out. Southern Chinese peasants, many with little or no restaurant experience, streamed into the business. By 1920 more than 11,000 Chinese were working as waiters, cooks, and restaurant operators. The field was now the largest employer of immigrants after the laundry business.

☆ ☆

Their food was a handy target for the animosity many still harbored for the Chinese. American Federation of Labor chief Samuel Gompers attacked the cuisine in a pamphlet, "Meat v. Rice: American Manhood Against Chinese Coolieism." Americans imagined the worst about the Chinese kitchen. "Contrary to the common impression, rats, cats, and puppies are no more commonly eaten by Chinese than by Americans," writer Wong Chin Foo reassured his *Cosmopolitan* readers in 1888.

To woo native diners, restaurateurs expanded their menu to include more reassuring items. The "Chinese-American" menu they contrived was made of cheap, quickly assembled, easily assimilated dishes. Egg foo yung, shrimp fried rice, spareribs, and sweet and sour pork were among the standbys. Chop suey and chow mein, a hash of fried noodles, meat and shrimp, and assorted vegetables crowned the list. Fortune cookies, which were probably invented by David Jung, an early twentieth-century Los Angeles noodle manufacturer, were a key part of the restaurant formula.

More than an appealing menu was necessary to attract customers. Chinatown's unsavory reputation was a formidable barrier. The quarters in San Francisco and other cities were attracting ruffians, "laboring classes and outlaws," one guidebook called them, drawn to the whorehouses, gambling dens, and opium joints. The vice trade sparked violence that scared off family and tourist business. Wars between the hatchet men of rival tongs or syndicates, robberies in gambling halls, and street crimes often erupted. "When seeing Chinatown especially at night it is advisable to go in the company of some friend who understands the heathen's ways or with a policeman," warned a guidebook to southern California.

Others shunned the districts because they feared filth and disease. An 1890 San Francisco guidebook warned readers about the leprosy that was scarring Chinatown. Disease-ridden beggars, the guide cautioned, were polluting the street corners. The "stale odors, sprawling drunks, overturned garbage cans, and giant rats" repelled a visitor to the neighborhood.

The merchants mobilized to drive out the crime bosses. Beginning in the late nineteenth century, they enlisted police to crack down on the vice and violence. Police raided gambling dens and houses of prostitution and stationed patrolmen to protect visitors. By the 1930s, the cleanup campaign was paying dividends. The businessmen, who now held sway over America's Chinatowns, were turning the communities into tourist districts. San Francisco's Chinatown, writer Pardee Lowe observed in 1936, had become the "chief jewel in San Francisco's starry diadem of tourist attractions."

In a safer, more appetizing setting, respectable restaurants, curio shops, and cocktail lounges garnered increasing numbers of new patrons. Celebrations on Chinese New Year and other occasions brought in crowds of visitors. The once tawdry neighborhoods acquired more inviting facades as Chinatown chambers of commerce promoted a pagoda style of architecture.

A spruced-up Chinatown, some entrepreneurs decided, could support more lavish eating establishments. Johnny Kan, a businessman who was raised in the gold-mining country, opened San Francisco restaurants that he hoped would be alluring to "Caucasians." Constructed to evoke a Ming or Tang dynasty, they were overseen by a staff of maître d's, hosts, and hostesses. Formality and elegance, he hoped, would distinguish his businesses from the "papa mama, medium size, juke and soup joints, tenderloin joints and others—where the waiters just slammed the dishes on the table."

Canning Bean Sprouts: Jeno Paulucci and Chun King

An unlikely figure, a Minnesota-born huckster of Italian ancestry, transformed chop suey and chow mein into popular supermarket items in post–World War II America. He taught millions of house-wives that canned and frozen Chinese food would make a satisfying family dinner.

Luigino Francesco Paulucci was born in 1918 in Aurora, one of the "locations" on the Minnesota Iron Range where immigrant laborers clus-tered. His father, Ettore, a northern Italian from Pesaro east of Florence, toiled thirteen hours for a daily wage of $4.20—when he had work. He suffered daily insults, such as being called a "dirty little wop," and re-turned home "bathed in red iron dust," Jeno recalls in his autobiography.

The living conditions were squalid. "I remember a tiny $5 a month four-room flat full of cockroaches that scurried for cover when you turned on the single bare light bulb," Jeno remembers. And "clouds of choking dust . . . billowed up from the road outside whenever the mining superintendent or assistant passed by in their chauffeur-driven limousines."

Young Jeno unloaded coal cars at a lumberyard. The youth scav-enged for coal along the railroad tracks that led into the mines. He loaded the pieces into a little red wagon that he had made from dis-carded parts and carted them home to fuel the family stove. To make ends meet, the family brewed wine in the basement that they sold by the glass or bottle to their customers. Constant police raids forced the family to move frequently.

The Pauluccis left Aurora and moved in 1924 to Hibbing, home to the world's largest open mine. During the summers, the youth, who began calling himself Jeno, sold tourists vials of different-colored ore that he had pilfered from the mine. He also helped his parents run a grocery store in the front room of their house.

A natural pitchman, Jeno worked for a local supermarket hawking fruit outside the shop. Impressed with his talent, the owner sent Jeno to the chain's flagship Duluth store for the summer. Standing on top of a wooden platform in front of the grocery, the young boy "was ready to yell my lungs out" to lure buyers. He battled a younger but bigger barker who shouted his spiel at a rival store across the street. The noise was so loud that Duluth passed an ordinance outlawing this kind of outdoor peddling. Jeno was already a shrewd merchandiser. When he received eighteen crates of bananas that had turned brown because of ammonia spray but were perfectly edible, the salesman promoted them as Argentine bananas. In three hours all the fruit was gone.

The sixteen-year-old was at a crossroads. He had been squeezing in his studies, most recently pre-law courses at junior college, between various jobs. The sales itch was too strong: He left school to go to work for a St. Paul wholesale grocery as a salesman for the northern regions of Michigan, Wisconsin, and Minnesota. Sleeping in his car, subsisting on canned meat, sardines, and other samples, Jeno hawked his products. In the process, he became a keener salesman. To sell canned peaches and pears, he put up store displays complete with catchy banners and signs. To commemorate National Canned Fruit Week, his invention, Jeno persuaded grocers to order his products.

Thirsting for more commercial adventure, Jeno left the wholesaler and moved back to Duluth. Fascinated by dehydrated garlic, he went on the road several days a week selling it to groceries. He supported himself working at his old grocery job and as a timekeeper in the shipyards. Jeno soon gave up on his product: "How much garlic could anybody use? A little goes a long way."

On one of his sales trips, Jeno discovered the bean sprout. In Minneapolis he found a group of Japanese growing bean sprouts in indoor gardens. After a few days, the mung beans sprouted in large crocks and vats of water and grew into delectable shoots. Unaffected by changes in the weather and not reliant on the soil, hydroponic gardening appealed to Jeno. He was confident that he could sell bean sprouts to restaurants, which were clamoring for fresh vegetables because of wartime rationing. Jeno threw himself into growing bean sprouts. He tried punching a washtub full of holes and waited for the plants to sprout. The experiment failed because he used soybeans instead of mung beans.

Determined to succeed, he borrowed $2,500 from Anthony Papa, an Italian food broker, and started a bean-sprout venture with David Pasha, a former partner. He recruited Japanese gardeners and sold sprouts in cellophane bags and bushel baskets to groceries and restaurants. He enticed housewives with recipes and brochures touting his product as rich in vitamins and minerals.

Jeno decided to produce bean sprouts on a larger scale. He found a pea cannery in Poplar, Wisconsin, that let him use the plant during the winter months. All he needed was a large supply of cans. Representing himself as an official of the Bean Sprout Growers Association, he convinced the War Production Board to give him a half million obsolete cans.

Forced to stop manufacturing in May when pea canning resumed, he was desperate for a facility to churn out bean sprouts year-round. He bought another pea plant in Iron River, Minnesota, for $5,000. When the factory burned down at the end of the war, Jeno acquired an old Quonset hut, which had been used for canning rutabagas, in Grand Rapids, Michigan.

Canning bean sprouts led to making chop suey, in which sprouts were a critical component. Jeno envisioned a huge market: "With so many young men returning from the far corners of the world I was sure that the exotic food business was going to be a growth industry." GIs who had fought in the Pacific, he was convinced, would be receptive to Chinese food. Cans of chop suey vegetables—bean sprouts cooked with celery, pimentos, and other ingredients—were the next items in his developing product line. Chow mein soon followed. Jeno sold his merchandise under the Foo Young brand name.

No fan of Chinese food, he wanted his foods to have a uniquely tangy flavor. "I realized that most of the Oriental foods that one gets in cans and in restaurants is a pretty bland sort of thing. I wanted something with verve, spicier than most Italian foods." Jeno asked his mother, Michelina, who was an excellent cook, for help. Michelina, who had sold spaghetti from her home, enlivened chop suey and chow mein recipes with Italian spices. The flavoring startled some in the food industry. "How do you expect to sell it with those peppers (sweet red) in it?" one regional buyer for a New England supermarket chain asked Jeno.

Dissatisfied with the Foo Young label, Jeno sought to conjure up a new brand name. He found one quite accidentally. As he tells the story, Jeno brought an order for chow mein labels to a Duluth printing firm. When the printer asked him what name he wanted on them, Jeno blurted out Chungking, which was then the capital of China. When the printer advised that "you will never be able to get a copyright on that one," Jeno decided to drop the "g" and use two words—Chun King—on the label. He liked its "rich imperial sound."

The company abandoned the Quonset hut and opened its own plant in Duluth in 1951. The Orient Express, the Chun King truck line, carted in shrimp from the Gulf, celery from Michigan, Florida, and California, and bamboo shoots and water chestnuts from Asia to make an expanding number of products. The business rolled out soy sauce, fortune cookies, egg rolls, and frozen TV dinners.

Because of Jeno's canny marketing, Chun King became the country's largest manufacturer of Chinese foods. He tinkered obsessively with the packaging of his products to increase their salability. He instructed his plant to can the meat and vegetables in chop suey separately because the raw materials had different cooking times. Chun King began selling chop suey meat and vegetables in a "Divider Pak," one of the earliest uses of this device. In another gimmick, he attached a can of noodles to a can of chow mein and offered the product in a two-for-one sale. Chop suey and chow mein were also packed in family-size cans, which were stacked up in tall, arresting displays.

The promoter assiduously plotted in-store displays to boost sales. Supermarkets were lavishly decorated for three festivals, summer Luau, the Fall Moon festival, and Chinese New Year, which together contributed a third of the company's yearly volume. Shops were decked out with lanterns and banners, pagodas, and rickshaws. Employees wearing conical-shaped "coolie" hats greeted shoppers. "Fork sticks" and "knife sticks" were given out as half-price premiums.

Jeno built up his business by calling on clients directly. Sometimes he needed all his ingenuity to save an account. Once he flew to Philadelphia to keep Food Fair, Chun King's first large supermarket customer, from dropping the line. To demonstrate the quality of his chop suey, Jeno remembers, he opened a can for the grocery's top buyer. Pulling up the lid to block the view, he extracted a grasshopper from the can and ate it before the buyer noticed. "This looks so delicious that I think I'll have the first bite myself," Jeno said. He kept the account.

Chun King was an innovator in using television ads to sell ethnic food. Gary Moore and Arthur Godfrey pushed its wares on their daytime programs in the 1950s. Jeno later hired comedian Stan Freberg to develop commercials. In one of his earliest and most memorable spots, the announcer said: "Nine out of ten doctors recommend Chun King chow mein." The camera then panned to a picture of ten beaming doctors in white coats, nine of whom were Chinese.

Another ad pictured a smiling housewife. In the background, a voice rang out: "Could it or couldn't it be Chun King Chow Mein? Only her grocer knows." Chun King was pitching to harried women shoppers. Its message—they needn't feel guilty about taking a shortcut and making dinner with the company's convenient and tasty products.

The advertising and marketing campaigns paid off. Sales soared from $500,000 in 1949 to $50 million ten years later. Jeno soon grew restless and began looking for new projects. In 1966 he sold Chun King to R. J. Reynolds for $63 million. A year later, he launched Jeno's, a frozen pizza company. Luigino's, his most recent venture, sells frozen Chinese and Italian entrées under the Yu Sing and Michelina's brand names. Looking back on his career, Jeno exulted: "Only in America would it be possible for a man with a name like Jeno Francesco Paulucci, son of poor Italian immigrants, to get rich selling Chinese food in a Scandinavian region."

East Meets East: The New Chinatown

This was no standard Chinese menu. Frothy, icy watermelon, honey-dew, papaya, mango, kiwi, and other fruit juices and shakes were of-fered. Young coconut, lychee, and longan drinks evoked the tropical East. The drinks lured diners who remembered these pleasures from their torrid homelands in South China and Southeast Asia.

Sweets were melded with starches from Southeast Asia. The restau-rant served fresh fruit, ice cream, and sago, a Malay word for the meal extracted from the trunk of palm trees. Fresh fruit could be ordered ei-ther with sago or tapioca pearls, the glutinous starch extracted from the cassava roots that the restaurant's owner called "tropical rice."

The hot dishes also seemed out of place. Taro pot, a house specialty, had as its centerpiece a "basket" made from the ancient Asian tuber, which is eaten very much like a potato. The taro ringed a delectable mixture of carrots, roasted peanuts, snow peas, and stir-fried shrimp, scallops, and squid. As a visitor worked his way through the crispy rim of the bowl to the tender morsels inside, the owner and waitress ar-gued about the lineage of the dish. It was definitely Malay, the wait-ress said. No, her boss insisted, it was Chinese.

Both were right. Taro's roots could be traced to either China or Southeast Asia. The dish is enjoyed equally in China and Malaysia. The Pearl Villa restaurant in Boston's Chinatown was a cultural hy-brid. It offered both Chinese and Malaysian dishes as well as entrées that married the two cuisines. The eatery epitomized a different kind of Chinatown, one with a distinctly Southeast Asian flavor.

Unlike the timid Chinese restaurants of old, the Villa served up un-varnished Cantonese food. Conspicuously absent were dishes drown-ing in gravy and heavy with cornstarch. Simple steamed fish was accented with soy, ginger, and spring onions. Watercress was delicately stir-fried. Lightly battered salty squid that had the bite of red pepper was served with *choy sum*, a tasty cabbage that bears yellow flowers when young. The light crust of the exquisitely fried scallops slipped off, offering up the succulent meat inside.

The eatery was equally comfortable preparing Southeast Asian curries. It turned out Singapore Noodle, a stir-fry of rice noodles, shrimp, pork, green onions, and bits of scrambled eggs, that was studded with green chilies. The noodles tinted yellow with turmeric were redolent of curry.

The Villa's voluminous menu catered to the varied tastes of Chinese immigrants. Dishes spanned the range of cooking styles, from Hong Kong and Cantonese to Szechuan and Shanghainese. Selections ran from soups, porridge, and fried noodles to baked spaghetti and macaroni. It included unexpected items like french toast, spam and egg sandwiches, and toast with peanut butter and jam. "The menu is so big," the owner noted, to give his customers "whatever they want."

The restaurant attracts both the Chinese old guard and young ethnic sophisticates. A festive party of hiply dressed college students, one wearing a Tommy Hilfiger shirt, sat around a banquet table on black lacquered chairs. A watercolor of a golden fish decorated the dusty green dining room. On their way out of the restaurant, a group of Chinese Generation-Xers wearing knapsacks trooped past fish tanks filled with lobster and crabs and one brimming with slithering eels.

The Pearl Villa occupied one of the nineteenth-century Greek revival–style row houses whose ground floors had been converted into Chinese restaurants and whose upper floors turned into sleeping quarters for workers in the late 1920s and 1930s. The basement now housed a cellular and paging shop and the Elegance of Asia hair salon. Next door was the KT and T travel agency, which offered a one-day bus trip to New York, no doubt to Chinatown, for $15.

Across the street from the restaurant stood the Peach Tree Seafood Restaurant, a Chinese Masonic Lodge, the Sunshine travel agency, and a restaurant serving "Korean, Chinese, and Japanese" sushi. An auto-supply store, Uncle Leo's tailor shop, and Boston Kitchenware added variety to the commercial landscape.

Tyler intersected with Beach Street, Chinatown's main drag, which followed the route of the old elevated streetcar line. Beach teemed with food purveyors. A food court sold mung bean and lychee fruit slush, soybean milk, and "cold herbal tea." Eastern Live Poultry, a venerable Chinatown institution, marketed turkeys, roosters, capons, rabbits, ducks, and chickens. Chinese women hawked red, ripe skinned mangoes, green pea shoots, and bok choy in front of a grocery. A young man vended prickly skinned lychee fruit, which he proclaimed as "very sweet, very delicious."

Durian, a thorny, football-shaped fruit native to Malaysia, was stacked in boxes near the vendors. The "king of fruits," whose name derives from *duri*, the Malay word for "spike," has rich, creamy flesh that can be used for ice cream and milk shakes. Southeast Asians swear to its powers as a remedy for stomach ills and as an aphrodisiac. On a street corner, two partners peddled a truckload of watermelons, a favorite summer treat of the Chinese, who like to nibble on the fruit's black seeds. "They go quick, 300 an hour," one vendor said.

Bakeries that often doubled as coffee shops filled Beach and the surrounding streets. Café patrons peered through the windows of these immigrant havens at passersby. The shops sold uniquely Chinese pastries, which are both sweet and savory. Mix Bakery on Beach, owned by a Hong Kong businessman, sells melon cakes filled with melon seeds and sesame seeds, which are popular wedding gifts, and giant walnut cookies. Sweet red bean pastry is another attraction. The bakery also carries products like sponge cakes, for those with more Western tastes.

All the bakeries offer moon cakes, which commemorate the autumn harvest festival that falls on the eighth month of the lunar calendar. The cake, now sold year-round, is variously made with black beans, lotus seeds, ham, dates, apricots, and a range of other fillings.

☆ ☆

America's third-largest Chinatown, a short walk from the Boston Common, the downtown shopping district, and other tourist attractions, is
located in an area that was once called South Cove. South Cove, the
southern part of the Boston peninsula, was built in the early 1800s from
the landfill of tidal flats. The area was constructed for middle-class Yan-
kees, who remained there through the 1850s. They were succeeded by
the Irish, who began moving into South Cove in the 1840s. New arrivals, Syrian Christians and Jews, drawn by jobs in leather and garment
factories, flowed in during the next several decades.

A small group of Chinese immigrants converged on the South
Cove in the late nineteenth century. One band came from North
Adams, a western Massachusetts mill town, where they had been
hired as strike breakers to crush a walkout from the Sampson Shoe
Factory. After the strike, 160 Chinese drifted to Boston, where they
pitched their tents near the corner of Essex and Oxford Streets. They
called their site Ping-On-Alley (Alley of Peace and Settlement).

They were joined by seventy-five immigrants from the West Coast
who had been recruited to build a telephone exchange near South Station. By 1890 the nucleus of what would become Chinatown consisted of 200 settlers and fifteen shops. The colony grew with the arrival of more immigrants who found work in textile and leather
factories, laundries, and Chinese restaurants, which sprang up in the
1920s. European immigrants began moving away from the area as a
predominantly Chinese district was being established.

Like California's early Chinese immigrants, South Cove's settlers
were peasant bachelors who mostly hailed from Toishan in southern
China and spoke the Cantonese dialect of that area. Jammed into
lodging houses, the single men expected to stay only temporarily before returning with a nest egg to their villages. Many gave up on the
dream, settled down, and never returned. When the U.S. laws barring
female immigrants from China were repealed after World War II,
more women joined the male enclave.

Beginning in the 1970s, an infusion of new immigrants would reshape the cloistered quarter. A new immigration law opened the door

to a surge of Asian settlers and encouraged family members to join their immigrant relatives. In Chinese lingo, the FOBs (fresh off the boat) began crowding in on the ABCs (American-born Chinese).

In a pattern that would be duplicated across Chinese America, the newcomers, in sharp contrast to the peasant pioneers, were frequently middle class and urbanized. Many had migrated from South China to Hong Kong, a way station in their passage to America. The Hong Kong émigrés, a Westernized group that included successful businessmen and professionals, were also conversant in English.

Waves of new settlers were also leaving Chinese outposts in Southeast Asia for enclaves in Boston and other cities. Like the Cantonese immigrants, their roots were in coastal South China, the traditional jumping-off point, but from different regions. They came from a long migratory tradition. For several generations their forefathers had been shipping out for the Nanyang (the Southern Ocean) in quest of opportunities in Southeast Asia. Fujian, a poor maritime province, which lay next to Kwangtung, the homeland of the Cantonese, produced many of the wayfarers. "Circled by mountains and girdled by the sea," as the saying went, it was separated from Taiwan by a narrow strait.

The "sea was paddy" to the passionate sailors and fishermen of the province. The Hokkien (the name of the people and their language) pioneered the junk trade to the Malacca Straits on the Malay peninsula. The voyagers built tight-knit settlements organized around common family names and village origins in the coastal cities of the region, first in Malacca, then Penang, and finally Singapore. After the British colonized the Straits in the early nineteenth century, Hokkien immigration grew rapidly. Many were corralled by the English to work the tin and rubber plantations and to fill the menial jobs that locals rejected. "Refugees from official displeasure . . . banishees from their local communities . . . free emigrants seeking their fortune, and . . . contract coolies were among the motley assortment," anthropologist Maurice Freedman observed. The Hokkien and their children would prosper in business and trade.

The Teo Chiu, another seafaring people, lived in northeastern Kwangtung, at the border of Fujian. The inveterate migrants sailed from Swatow, a busy port, for Southeast Asia to improve their lot. Eyes were painted on the bows of their boats. "The people of the tidelands" shared customs with the Hokkien and spoke a dialect similar to theirs.

The Teo Chiu, who would also migrate to the Straits, were most numerous in Vietnam and Thailand. They gradually rose from lowly stations to become a powerful class. An eighteenth-century Thai king was the son of a Thai mother and a Teo Chiu father. Entrepreneurial occupations were their preference. In Vietnam's Cholon (large market), the Chinese trading center outside Saigon, they controlled the rice business.

The Chinese in Southeast Asia suffered from the persecutions of hostile governments and nationalist movements that arose in the 1950s and 1960s. Seeking new homes that would provide peace and security and a more favorable climate for business, many ethnic Chinese left for America. Boston was an attractive destination for the twice-resettled migrants.

A polyglot Chinatown was now forming, bringing together Cantonese, Hong Kong Chinese, Chinese exiles from Southeast Asia, and people from mainland Chinese cities like Shanghai and Peking. The residents spoke different tongues—Toishanese, Cantonese, Teo Chiu, Hokkien, Hakka. The quarter was once again a beachhead for sojourners, who planned to leave the cramped neighborhood as soon as they had established themselves.

This Chinatown was taking on a new role, that of cultural and commercial capital serving a far-flung community. Advertisements on a Beach Street bulletin board for homes in Westboro, Quincy, and Attleboro were signs of a budding Chinese suburbia. Suburban dwellers, who drove into Boston to shop and dine on dim sum, expanded the neighborhood's commercial base. Chinese visitors from other parts of the Northeast and from abroad also thronged the New England ethnic center.

☆ ☆

The newcomers changed the face of Chinatown. Entrepreneurs cleaned up the area, renovated properties, and opened new businesses. In the late 1970s, Hong Kong businessman David T. Wong set his sights on the seedy Combat Zone, a six-block section of sex clubs, peep shows, and other "adult" businesses, which hemmed in Chinatown. He rented to Vietnamese noodle shops and a Chinese grocery and built a 1,500-seat upscale restaurant on the premises of the former Pussycat Cinema. More Hong Kong expatriates financed new businesses. The changes brought more visitors to the quarter. A growing number of diners, including theater patrons from the adjacent district, were spending their dollars in the enticing neighborhood.

The Chinese diaspora from Southeast Asia transplanted distinctive foods and flavors. Ethnic Chinese from Vietnam ran a large share of Chinatown's restaurants. Vietnamese script proclaimed their specialties. *Pho,* the savory rice-noodle soup laced with ginger, cinnamon, and fish sauce, was a staple of the eateries. The traditional breakfast repast, which had originated in Hanoi and spread to the South, was catching on with nonethnics. The soup was available in many venues—a sign on a fabric shop advertising it beckoned to passersby.

Grand Chau Chau. Chau Chow City. The restaurants with the puzzling names announced the presence of the Teo Chiu in Chinatown. The Luu family, a large ethnic Chinese clan that had been in the fertilizer business in Vietnam, launched Chau Chow, their first restaurant, in 1985 on Beach Street. Benny Luu, who had been scraping by as a dishwasher, and a chef-partner "wanted to distinguish their food from other local restaurants," Benny's son, Clayton, remarked.

The small family-style operation with a mostly ethnic clientele was followed by Grand Chau Chow, which the Luus opened across the street in 1990. The larger establishment was a "more upscale, tablecloth," restaurant, Clayton Luu noted. Striped bass, lobster, shrimp, crab, and abalone swam in its trademark fish tank. Chau Chow City, a three-story banquet house specializing in dim sum, which opened in

1997, was the acme of the family's achievements. American and Asian customers, particularly Vietnamese, hold their weddings in the restaurant.

The Luus did not want to confine their businesses to Chinatown. They started a chain of Super 88 supermarkets, which were located in South Bay and other sections of the city (88 signifies wealth to the Chinese). A relative has recently created two new seafood restaurants on the Boston pier, a popular tourist area.

Their developing menus highlight dishes that the Teo Chiu created in South China and Southeast Asia as well as more familiar Cantonese plates. They are adept at seafood specialties like clams in black bean sauce; minced prawns, crab, pork, and water chestnuts wrapped in bean curd; and oyster cake, a shellfish omelette. Instead of steamed rice, they prefer to serve *congee,* a thick rice porridge, mixed with chicken, beef, and abalone. Soy duck, a specialty, is draped in a sauce of stir-fried shrimp, scallops, and squid. *Sha cha* (tea sand) noodles, a Southeast Asian creation, are stir-fried in a sauce of chili, sesame, peanuts, and dried fish.

☆ ☆

Chinese food promoters in Boston, New York, San Francisco, Washington, and other cities are introducing Americans to Malaysian food, which was little known before the 1980s. The cuisine is a medley of influences from the Malay, Chinese, and Indian peoples of the region.

The union of male Chinese immigrants to the Straits, predominantly Hokkien, and Malay women resulted in a blending of their culinary traditions. The *Babas,* who were ambitious to become *towkays* (men of influence), married *nonyas* (women of means). The cuisine they fashioned was known as nonya.

Dishes combined such Chinese staples as pork, bean curd, bean sprouts, and soy with the spices and fragrances of Southeast Asia. Nonya foods had the punch of chili and the pungency of *blacan,* a paste made by pounding, salting, drying, and fermenting shrimp.

Dishes were imbued with the scent of lemon grass and coriander and with the sour flavors of green mango, lime leaves, and tamarind, the bean-shaped fruit with a sticky datelike filling in its pod. Coconut milk permeated curries and other dishes. The metamorphosis was so complete that Chinese food in Southeast Asia "doesn't taste Chinese anymore," Eric C. C. Lin, the owner of a pioneering Chinese-Indonesian restaurant in Washington, points out.

Noodles, a Chinese import that the Hokkien especially loved, were incorporated in stir-fries and soups sold first in outdoor stalls and more recently in modernized food courts. Noodles were adopted by the Malays, who gave them the Chinese name, *mee. Laksa,* a tart and spicy noodle soup, unites the Chinese and Malay styles. Rice-flour noodles akin to spaghetti are cooked in a rich coconut-milk broth of fish or shrimp, bean sprouts, and tofu. Chili, ginger, tamarind, and lemon grass invigorate the soup.

Customers pour into Penang, a Malaysian food palace in Boston's Chinatown housed in what had once been a strip club, to sample a panorama of food combinations. The restaurant, owned by an ethnic Chinese business group, intrigues diners with a moist Indian flat bread from Malaysia that they dip in chicken curry. The dish's name, *roti canai,* is Hindi. *Satay,* an appetizer of strips of grilled chicken or beef, probably a legacy of Arab traders to Southeast Asia, arrives with a peppery peanut sauce.

Another favorite dish, *popiah* (thin pastry), resembles a spring roll. But the *popiah* was invented by Hokkien settlers in Malaysia. It is an uncooked wrapper filled with shrimp, bamboo shoots, bean sprouts, and jicama, a crispy root vegetable sometimes known as the yam bean, whose taste lies somewhere between a potato and an apple. Daubed with stripes of chili and black bean sauce, the Southeast Asian Chinese treat has become a fixture of the Malay table.

Penang's *chow kueh tow* is another dish whose Hokkien name has seeped into the Malay vocabulary. Flat rice noodles are stir-fried in a wok with shrimp, squid, bean sprouts, and chives. Soy and chili paste season this street-market standard.

At the Pearl Villa, a Chinese-Malaysian restaurant, the chef produced a beef curry whose name, *rendang,* had a deliciously evocative ring. The West Sumatran dish, originally made with water buffalo, traveled to Malaysia. Slowly simmered, the beef absorbs the chili-infused coconut-milk gravy.

Hainan chicken, another menu listing, is a Malaysian classic made by Chinese cooks from the island, which is off the southernmost tip of Kwangtung province. Immigrants from the tropical isle of palm and coconut trees opened cafés and coffee shops in Malaysia in the nineteenth and twentieth centuries. The dish, which they conjured up in their new land, is a platter of cold, tender slices of steamed chicken flavored with a soy marinade. It comes with dipping sauces of ginger and green chili and red chili.

The Villa's Singapore Noodle, the curried rice stick noodle stir-fry, is mystifying. The dish made its way to Hong Kong from Southeast Asia and has since been transported to America by Chinese and Malaysian restaurateurs. This "spaghetti Eastern" marries Chinese ingredients like pork and noodles with the flavorings enjoyed by Indian immigrants, who had been brought to Malaysia as indentured laborers. Perplexing to a Westerner, the combination seems perfectly sensible to the Chinese. "Singapore, China, same thing," a Hong Kong chef once told me.

CHAPTER 6

....

Currying Favor:
Indian and Pakistani Food

Across the Great Divide:
Indian Cooking of the North and South

KEBABS, *BIRYANIS, PILAUS, KORMAS, SAMOSAS.* Surprisingly, many of the hallmarks of the Indian restaurant are dishes that are not commonly eaten by the majority of that country's immigrants to the United States. These dishes are Muslim in origin, whereas most Indians are Hindus. Indian cooking in America bears the distinctive imprint of the Islamic conquerors of North India.

It was a royal cuisine that the Moghuls, the most important of these colonizers, brought from their Central Asian homeland. They infused it with Persian techniques and incorporated the local seasonings and raw materials of the Indian subcontinent. The culinary style became the standard that the region's cooks and restaurateurs strove to emulate.

When Indian cooking was exported to America, it was this grand Muslim tradition that held sway in North Indian restaurant dining rooms. The specialties might be denatured, but the dominance of the cuisine was undeniable. From the menu items to the evocative names of the establishments—Taj Mahal, Akbar, Peacock, Bukhara—that conjured up the glories of the Moghul age, the restaurants were serv-

115

ing up a one-dimensional image of Indian food. Even the earliest popularizers of Indian cooking in America stressed North Indian dishes. In *An Invitation to Indian Cooking*, the first and most widely read of these primers, Madhur Jaffrey tells her readers that she has emphasized the food of Delhi, the Moghul capital, and its surrounding area. Until quite recently, then, the culinary diversity of a nation with wide variations in climate, language, religion, and topography was reduced to a single cooking style.

To understand the allure of this imperial cuisine, you must transport yourself to the Moghul epoch, to the beginnings of a dynasty that lorded over North India from 1526 to 1858. The Moghul ruler, Tamerlane, who commanded these nomadic Turks, built a vast empire that stretched over Central Asia, including much of India and Afghanistan. The world he ruled from his capital in Samarkand, in present-day Uzbekistan, was influenced by Persian culture, and the coarser Moghuls adopted the more refined Persian customs and values, learned that language, and converted to Islam.

Babur, a descendant of both Tamerlane and Genghis Khan, led his troops south after a rival tribe, the Uzbeks, wrested control of Samarkand. Like many earlier invaders who swooped down from the steppes and through the mountainous Hindu Kush, the warriors marched through the Punjab and overpowered Northern India. Emperor Babur set out to civilize India, to reshape it in the image of the Persian and Central Asian culture he revered. He grumbled about the primitive manners and the mediocre amenities of the colony:

> Hindustan is a place of little charm. There is no beauty in its people, no graceful social intercourse, no poetic talent or understanding, no etiquette, nobility, or manliness. The arts and crafts have no harmony or symmetry. There are no good horses, meat, grapes, melons, or other fruit. There is no ice, cold water, good food, or bread in the markets. There are no baths and no Madrasas. There are no candles, torches, or candlesticks.

Homesick for the fruits and nuts of his homeland, Babur recruited gardeners from Afghanistan and Persia to plant melons, peaches, apricots, figs, pistachios, walnuts, and almonds. His successors erected mosques, forts, palaces, and tombs, such as the Taj Mahal, creating a landscape of Persian architectural splendor. Patrons of Persian culture, they fostered painting, music, and poetry and adopted Persian as the official language of the kingdom.

The Moghuls displayed their power ostentatiously. A golden peacock with a tail of blue sapphire and a breast of ruby was sculptured over the canopy of the throne. Emperor Akbar reveled in his possessions, a sixteenth-century traveler reported: "The king hath 100 elephants, 30,000 horses, 1,400 tame deer, 800 concubines, and other such store of leopard, tiger, buffalos, cock and hawks that it is very strange to see."

The cultural life of the Moghuls revolved around the palace, where the royal kitchens fashioned their opulent cuisine, modeled on Persian food but also drawing on Turkish roots. Four hundred cooks laid out 500 dishes a day for Akbar, his 300 wives, and entourage. The kitchen was stocked with jewel-studded ladles and expensive Ming porcelain to serve the most regal dishes. From Delhi, the capital, Moghul cooking filtered down to the provinces, where rajahs, maharajahs, and generals imitated the imperial style.

The Moghuls, fierce warriors accustomed to slaughtering animals for their food, were ardent meat eaters. Dishes heavy with chicken, beef, and lamb did not violate their Islamic faith. Lamb was the crown jewel of the Moghul kitchen. *Rogan josh,* a fixture of today's Indian restaurant, epitomized the court cuisine. Sometimes called *shahi rogan josh* (red juice), it is a stew of cubed lamb suffused in a buttery tomato sauce seasoned with red chilies. Clarified butter, or ghee, was dear to the Moghuls, who considered it "food that feeds the brain." For a particularly special occasion, guests were served a decadent lamb roast; softened in yogurt, this *shahi raan* was studded with cashews, almonds, poppy seeds, and raisins.

Even chicken, the imperial second choice, was given a royal touch. *Murgh makhani,* the ancestor of the "butter chicken" of Indian restaurant repertoire, was redolent of rich oil, cream, and the tomato sauce in which it simmered.

The Moghuls also took the stews they learned from the Persians and made them richer, spicier, meatier, and more extravagant. *Korma,* which derives from the Turkish "to fry," was a braised dish, a sort of dry curry. Starting with a gravy made from sautéed onions, garlic, and ginger, cooks prepared a sauce laden with yogurt and cream and often thickened with powdered almonds, walnuts, and pistachios, nuts much enjoyed by the Persians. Sweet spices like cardamom, cinnamon, and cloves heightened the voluptuous flavoring that permeated the meat. *Korma* is now a mainstay of the Indian restaurant menu.

Lavish rice dishes were also a hallmark of Moghul cooking. Inspired by Persian techniques, cooks wove together rice, meats, nuts, dried fruits, and other materials into elegant compositions. Works of artistry, they were also deliciously aromatic. The *pilau* (or *pullao*), the child of the Persian *polo* and the parent of our rice pilaf, married meats, chicken or lamb, and long-grain rice grown in the Himalayan foothills. The plainer combination of Indian cooking, simple rice and lentils, was elevated into an offering whose intricacy impressed one English traveler: "Rice boiled so artificially that every grain lies singly without being added together, with spices intermingled and a boiled fowl in the middle."

The *pilau* was perfumed with cinnamon, cardamom, cloves, and other spices. Saffron gave the dish a radiant color and an attractive scent. Native to Iran, saffron was cherished by the Persians not only as a cooking ingredient but also as a dye, spice, and medicine. The Moghuls fell in love with saffron and brought it to India.

Pilaus could be sweet as well as savory. A celebratory dish named in honor of Babur's daughter, Gulrukh (Rose-Colored Princess), was fragrant with orange, rose essence, and saffron. A popular treat for weddings and feast days, it was decorated with almonds and rose petals.

Chefs vied to produce the most intricate and gorgeous *pilau*. In Lucknow, a center of Moghul culture in North India, a cook created a dish to resemble the brilliant seeds of the pomegranate, another passion of the Persians. He colored half of each rice grain ruby red and the other half a crystalline white.

A *moti pilau* was fashioned, Indian scholar and Lucknow native A. H. Sharar writes,

> to look as if the rice contained shining pearls. The method of making these pearls was to take about two hundred grams in weight of silver foil and twenty grams of gold foil and beat them into the yolk of an egg; this mixture was then stuffed into the gullet of a chicken and tied around with fine thread. The chicken was heated slightly and the skin cut with a penknife. Well-formed shining pearls appeared, which were cooked with the meat of the pilau.

The *biryani*, an intricate elaboration of the *pilau*, is layered rice and meat adorned with shredded onions, pistachios, almonds, raisins, and luminous with saffron. Another Persian legacy, its name comes from the word "to bake." The royal casseroles were served with a flourish, displayed on three- to four-foot gold and silver platters resplendent with sheets of edible silver foil.

During festive occasions, guests refreshed themselves with *sharbats*, luxurious sweet drinks of almond, orange, pomegranate, and lemon that were passed on to the Moghuls by the Persians. (The English word "sherbet" is derived from the Arabic word.) The drinks were cooled with ice and snow that the palace in Delhi sent horsemen to retrieve from the mountainous Hindu Kush. The offer of a frosty *sharbat* to a guest was considered a mark of hospitality. When the Moghul emperor Humayun arrived at the Persian court in 1544, Tahmasp, the country's shah, ordered that "upon his auspicious arrival let him drink fine sherbets of lemon and rosewater, cooled with snow."

Dinners often ended with plates of fruit that flourished in Central Asia. The emperors sated themselves on grapes from Kabul and melons from Samarkand.

Moghul cooking reached new heights in the Muslim city of Lucknow. Under the Nawabs, the city's rulers, Lucknow developed an aristocratic cuisine more opulent than that of Delhi's emperors. The city was renowned for skewered meats, especially the elegant *kakori* kebab, named for a town near Lucknow. Lamb shoulder was pounded relentlessly into a paste, into which were mixed powdered almonds, pistachios, and spices—saffron, cinnamon, cloves, and nutmeg. Kebabs were then molded in the shape of cigars, grilled, and served to an audience of *kabobi-sharabis*—Urdu for "discerning diners."

Breads prepared in a grand style were a signature of Lucknow cooking. Muslim cooks transformed *poori*, the basic fried bread of Indians, into a richer *paratha* by buttering the layers of dough with ghee. Lucknow bakers went a step further and made a *paratha* fragrant with cardamom. The *shirmal,* a fancy sweet bread reserved for weddings and other lavish celebrations, was the most elegant of Lucknow's baking productions. The flaky delicacy, invented by the owner of a food stall in the eighteenth century, was brushed with ghee and imbued with saffron milk (*sheer* is Persian for "milk").

Lucknow was also the capital of confectionery. Halvah, from the Arabic *halwa* for "sweets," was a gift to India from the migrating Muslims. Adorned with pistachios and almonds and flavored with saffron and cardamom, the ghee-rich desserts had all the trappings of the Moghul kitchen. For special occasions, sweets arrived at the table gilded with gold or silver leaf.

Moghul sweets, many with Persian or Arabic names, have become standard desserts in the Indian restaurant. *Barfi*, which comes from the Persian for "snow," is a fudgelike confection made from reducing milk to a solid. *Gulab jamun,* small balls shaped from thickened condensed milk, are fried in ghee and drenched in rose water (*gulab* is Persian for "rose"). Spirals of dough that have been fried and permeated with a syrup of saffron and rose water, the multicolored *jalebi* were known as *zalabia* in Arabic.

Lucknow's *halvae* (sweet makers) had a penchant for excess. Madhur Jaffrey discovered a recipe for one such extravagance: [T]ake the yolks of a hundred eggs. Add equal quantities—in weight—of *ghee* . . . milk and sugar. Stir and cook gently until the halva becomes grainy like semolina. Add fine shavings of almonds and pistachios and spread out in a tray. Cool a bit and cut into squares or diamonds.

☆ ☆

Few Indian restaurants in the United States duplicate the dazzle of Moghul cooking. Far too often these dishes are stripped of their elegance and complexity and added to a homogenized North Indian menu of curries, tandooris, and kebabs. The builders of the standard Indian restaurant in America usually were not Indian immigrants but Bangladeshi and other Muslim newcomers.

Bangladeshi immigrants in New York City have carved out a restaurant niche as purveyors of reasonably priced North Indian food that is virtually interchangeable from one eatery to the next. The entrepreneurs, whose homeland's diet is based on rice and fish, serve their patrons from a menu heavy in lamb and chicken. As Muslims, though, the Bangladeshis have none of the compunctions about preparing meat that have kept many Indian Hindus out of the restaurant business.

A group of six Bangladeshi brothers who lived in the East Village in the late 1960s pioneered these ventures. The family members, some of whom studied at New York University and other colleges while the others held jobs, were homesick for their native food. They found a Japanese restaurant for sale on East Sixth Street, purchased it for $2,000, and converted it into a communal kitchen.

Passersby assumed that the people gathered there were eating in a restaurant, Manir Ahmed, one of the brothers, told a *New York Times* reporter. "People kept knocking on the door or walking in thinking we were a restaurant. So we thought maybe we should open a restaurant." Shah Bagh, their first enterprise, opened soon thereafter with Manir as owner and his brother, Moin, as cook. Indian food became popular in a neighborhood whose nonconformist atmosphere attracted students, artists, bohemians, and followers of Eastern religions.

The family was not satisfied with one restaurant. "We wanted to make an Indian street," Manir Ahmed said. "Very quickly we make good money cooking for Americans." A network of eateries was soon assembled. Brother Hasib took the helm of Kismoth in 1972, and the Nishan, Anar Bagh, Shamoly, and other curry houses soon sprang up, run by one of the brothers or their kin.

The success of the Ahmed clan encouraged other businessmen to emulate them. Twenty years later, the original restaurants had departed, but more than twenty-five Bangladeshi-owned dining rooms with names like Rose of India, Gandhi, and Sonali stretched out along the block of Sixth Street between First and Second Avenues. The competition is still heated, with restaurant barkers pitching their fare to passersby. Although some of the signs advertise both Indian and Bangladeshi cooking, the restaurants are basically marketing Indian food. Khalimir Rahmen Chowdury, owner of the Raj Mahal, explained his strategy: "Bangladesh is a small country. India is famous. That's why it's an Indian restaurant." Mohammed Habib, the assistant manager of the Rose of India, elaborated: "I think it should be 'Rose of Bangladesh,' but it's a business step. We are known as Indian people."

Restaurant menus, with slight variations, imitate one another. A litany of North Indian standards—*kormas, masalas, biryanis*—dominate the bill of fare. From a few basic sauces, kitchens assemble a roster of curries like *madras* (hot) and *vindaloo* (very hot) that differ from each other by small degrees of flavor, spice, and fire. The Curry Lane restaurants are so uniform that they have spawned an urban legend: They all shared a common kitchen, the story went.

The Bangladeshi restaurant empire today extends far beyond the East Village. "I'd say 95 percent of New York's Indian restaurants belong to Bangladeshis," Akbar Chowdhury, a manager of Great India, an Upper East Side restaurant, told *New York Times* reporter Barbara Crossette. Most of the owners hail from Sylhet, a hilly tea- and rice-growing region in northeastern Bangladesh, whose people share a long tradition of migration. Eager to improve their condition, sons of peasant villagers journeyed forth, often to work on merchant ships in the British navy.

Some of the seamen, or "lascars," began settling in England in the 1920s and 1930s and opened cafés in London, Cardiff, Liverpool, and other port cities that catered to their fellow Muslims. These establishments, which started wooing a British clientele, were the ancestors of the country's high street (main street) curry houses, a business the Bangladeshis dominate. They copied one another's names and mimicked competitors' decor right down to the flocked wallpaper and dim lighting. The chefs manufactured a set of formulaic dishes that relied on "pots of various stocks and gravies, pre-prepared meat, fish and vegetables, plus spices and a drive to cut corners," a writer for the English restaurant guide *Time Out* commented.

As English immigration laws grew more restrictive, Bangladeshis set their sights on America. "And then in the early 1970s, gradually more people from Sylbet were coming to New York," Bangladeshi restaurateur Shamsher Wadud told Barbara Crossette. "They saw the opportunities in America. They thought they'd do well because they did well in England." The inexpensive Indian restaurant in New York City would soon resemble its London relative.

☆ ☆

Immigrants from other regions are breaking with the North Indian restaurant mold by asserting their own culinary identities. South Indian cooking springs from a culture radically different from that of the North. The folkways of the steamier, tropical South have more in common with Southeast Asia than they do with those in North India, which is closely linked to Central Asia. Its people, the darker-skinned

Dravidians, inhabited India for many centuries before the Moghuls and earlier invaders of the northern region transplanted their customs.

South India is more fervently Hindu than the North, which was more strongly shaped by Islam. Many North Indians eat meat; the South remains largely vegetarian. Southern meals are built around rice; Northern cooking relies more on wheat breads for its starches. On the "Southern side," as residents like to call it, curries are fierier than the more subdued Northern dishes. Tropical fruits—coconut, tamarind, guava—also figure more prominently in the Southern kitchen.

The basics of the Southern diet are produced from cereals and lentils, or dal, and other basic raw materials. From this rudimentary foundation, South Indian cooks have developed a repertoire of dishes every bit as complex as North India's. The most famous of the region's culinary inventions, a pancake called a *dosa,* has won a devoted following from American enthusiasts of vegetarian food.

The long crispy crepe is formed from a batter of rice flour and ground lentils that stands overnight. Poured on a griddle, it is fried to a golden brown. Rolled up, the slightly sour-tasting *dosa,* the result of fermentation, can be eaten plain or filled with curried potatoes and onions. The latter version and the most popular, the *masala dosa,* can be as long as two feet. The *rava dosa,* a variation of the *masala,* is a semolina and rice-flour crepe, filled with multicolored lentils and mustard seeds.

Dosai and other South Indian dishes are traditionally served with side dishes. They come with a spicy *sambar,* a soupy mix of pureed lentils and vegetables. Another accompaniment is coconut chutney, ground coconut accented with chilies and mustard seeds, which are ubiquitous in South Indian cooking. Dipping the *dosa* in these sauces is part of the dining ritual.

Produced from the same rice and dal batter as the *dosa* is the *idli,* a steamed, spongy dumpling. The batter is poured into circular trays of a specially designed steamer. The *idli* has the same distinctively sour fragrance as its relative. South Indian cooks also dreamed up a rice-

and lentil-flour omelette-like pancake, the *uthappam* ("fermented pancake" in Tamil). The snack gets its bite from the onions and chilies in the batter.

These items are often eaten for breakfast along with coffee, a popular South Indian beverage. They are ideal for *tiffin*, a light lunch, and are hawked throughout the day by street vendors and served in railway snack bars, restaurants, and cafés.

With boundless ingenuity, South Indian cooks have created imaginative rice dishes. Yogurt rice, soft rice suffused with milk and a few spoonfuls of yogurt and sparked with red chili, ginger, and mustard seeds, is a hot-weather favorite. Equally cooling is a tart dish made by mixing rice with the sour paste of tamarind, the bean-shaped tropical fruit.

Tamils and other ethnic groups from South India have brought their food to commercial enclaves ranging from New York City's Curry Hill to suburban Langley Park, Maryland. Purveyors of vegetarian food have set up shop along Oak Tree Road, the bustling Indian bazaar in Edison, New Jersey. South Indian restaurants have also sprung up in such unlikely places as Decatur, Georgia, and Santa Clara, California.

Vegetarian restaurants with names like Udipi Palace strike a nostalgic chord among the growing numbers of South Indian immigrants. Udipi, the capital of orthodox Brahman culture on the country's southwest coast, is home to the ancient Krishna temple and to monasteries that are magnets for visitors and pilgrims. The city's Brahmans learned vegetarian cooking by preparing meals for the many visitors. Udipi restaurants, which sprouted throughout South India, recruited experienced Brahman cooks. The eateries, which prepared *dosai, idlis,* and other staples of the vegetarian menu, gained a reputation for the cleanliness, purity, and quality of their food. The *masala dosa* they serve was reputedly invented in Udipi.

These eateries are also building a clientele among the well-traveled Peace Corps generation, who welcome an alternative to the meat-rich food of North India. Many of the same diners have developed a craving for healthful vegetarian cooking. The adventurous are discarding their older Indian restaurant vocabulary and delighting in the exotic sounds of *idli, uppuma,* and *uthappam.*

Kebab from Punjab

The BP Halal Market in Arlington, Virginia, courts customers with spices, sweets, and sanctified meats as well as with saris, Islamic books, and phone cards. The shop helps patrons convert their videos so they will play on American videocassette players. In suburban Washington, grocers and butchers sell whole goat, lamb, and sheep that have been slaughtered in the religiously approved *halal* method that Muslim adherents demand.

A host of businesses are marketing their products to a burgeoning influx of Pakistani immigrants. Accountants, attorneys, real estate agents, and mortgage companies reach out for clients from this community. Travel agencies, airlines, and immigration advisers advertise their services to its peripatetic population. Newspapers advertise package tours for Muslims making the hajj, or pilgrimage, to Mecca and Medina. Vendors of satellite television push their products to ethnics eager to keep up with news back home.

Shops cater to women trying to preserve their cultural traditions. Saris, fabrics, gold jewelry, and other ornaments are marketed widely. Zaib, a store in northern Virginia, bills itself as a "specialist in bridal makeup." Its boutique carries "wedding and party clothes for ladies."

These are the visible signs of a Pakistani community beginning to take root. The Muslim immigrants, who gravitated to the Virginia suburbs of Washington, D.C., separated from a well-established Indian community, which had already clustered on the other side of the city, in Maryland. Taxi drivers, grocers, and gas station owners, occupations of choice for many early immigrants, as well as doctors, engineers, computer specialists, and other professionals make up this colony. The largest group comes from Punjab, the wealthiest and most influential of Pakistan's states.

The Pakistanis brought with them their culinary culture. The kebab house, a combination café, snack bar, and meeting place, has been transplanted wherever the South Asians have produced a critical commercial mass. Since the mid-1990s, Shalimar, Charcoal Kebab, Village Kebab, Kebob Express, East-West Grill, and many other outlets in northern Virginia have raced to meet the demand. Like their counterparts in New York, Los Angeles, and Chicago, the Pakistani restaurateurs are also educating a mainstream audience in the pleasures of their barbecue.

The first Washington-area kebab houses, which often lacked a distinct ethnic identity, paved the way for the more recent, expressly Pakistani enterprises. The Food Factory was opened in the mid-1980s by a taxi driver who was born in Afghanistan but reared in Pakistan. Since it could not depend on an exclusively Pakistani clientele, the Arlington restaurant welcomed Afghani, Arab, Iranian, and Turkish customers.

An early advertisement pictured a *kebabi*, a cook dressed in traditional garb, holding a skewer of meat while watching barbecue cooking over a flaming grill. The Food Factory was wooing an audience that wanted familiar street food served up in a speedy fashion. The draw was *halal* chicken and lamb kebabs and piping hot nan, the long, flat bread that is ubiquitous in Central and South Asia.

Not far from the Food Factory in Crystal City, a high-rise suburb close to National Airport, the Kebab House was grilling meats and baking bread with an Afghan touch. The owner, an Afghani who had learned the restaurant business at a Popeye's Chicken franchise, was making a more lightly spiced kebab than the Pakistani version.

His customers were a mixed lot. Unable to make their bread at home, Afghanis bought nan to take out. A loyal group of Somali taxi drivers, who cruised the area, took eagerly to the kebab fare. In their homeland, roasting cow, lamb, and camel was customary, and *halal* meat was an inducement to these observant Muslims. Persians and a scattering of other Middle Easterners also frequented the shop. Occasional groups of American diners came to sample an unfamiliar cuisine. Although the restaurant tried to attract Pakistanis, they never became a sizable clientele.

Meanwhile, the Kebab Palace, a new eatery, was busily trying to lure Pakistanis to its premises a mile down the road from the Kebab House. The owner, though Afghanistan-born, had spent most of his life in Pakistan, an advantage he had over his nearby competitor. A plaque on the wall listed sayings from the Koran. A painting of horsemen riding in a mountainous terrain summoned up the Afghanistan frontier. Men wearing skullcaps and long flowing robes proceeded down the cafeteria line. The taxis parked outside were a telltale sign that these scouts of reasonably priced, filling food had discovered the Palace. Separated from their families, the single men found companionship and warmth in the café.

Although it was more Pakistani than the Kebab House, the Palace was a mélange of traditions. It offered the standard kebabs and nan (which the menu curiously called pita) favored by its Pakistani patrons, but it also dispensed Persian specialties—*kabob-e-kubideh,* a "ground sirloin" plate, and *sherazi* salad, a mixture of cucumbers, tomatoes, and onions dressed with olive oil and lemon. *Qabili,* an Afghan pilaf of basmati rice cooked with meat, carrots, and raisins, was another selection.

Persian kebab houses had been flourishing in the Washington, D.C., region. The most successful, Moby Dick, a chain named for a famous restaurant in Tehran, prepared kebab sandwiches on nan complete with lettuce, tomatoes, onions, and feta cheese as well as classic Persian kebabs, grilled meat served with elaborately prepared *chelo* (white rice). *Doogh,* a minty yogurt drink, was a favorite of the eatery's Iranian customers.

☆ ☆

Ravi Kabob House, a café that serves hearty bazaar food with a Punjabi accent in an informal, convivial setting, exemplifies the Pakistani-style kebab house. Opened on July 4, 1996, it is run by Mohammed

Afzal and his brother, Tariq, natives of Islamabad. Ravi is located in the Buckingham neighborhood of Arlington, Virginia. It is an area of garden apartments built during World War II, once mostly lower-middle-class white, that is now experiencing an influx of Bolivians, Salvadorans, Guatemalans, and other immigrants.

The small commercial strip in which Ravi is located is a crazy quilt of ethnic commerce. Among Ravi's neighbors are Cassiana Spa, an Asian salon offering massage, nail care, and waxing; Bangkok Siam, a Thai restaurant; Eastern Carry Out, a Chinese fast-food outlet selling chicken and subs; and Rincon Chapin, a Guatemalan luncheonette that sits in a spot long occupied by diners.

Posters for Pakistani concerts and other Islamic events hang on Ravi's door. A sign announces that the restaurant serves *halal* meat. A refrigerated display case containing skewers of chicken, lamb, and beef faces the small, informal dining area. Behind the counter, workers can be seen grilling meats, refilling curries on the steam table, and tending simmering stews. A cook rolls dough out onto a small pillow, sprinkles a little water on it, and slaps it against the side of the tandoor, the traditional clay oven.

A painting of Lahore's River Ravi, whose waters originate in the mountains of Kashmir, adorns the wall. Drawn by Tariq, an accomplished artist as well as a cook, it depicts a tranquil setting. Water buffalo graze on the shore and swim in the waters. Boats line the riverbank. The River Ravi strikes a deep chord with his customers, Tariq says. "Lahore people know Ravi."

The walls of the famous Lahore Fort, built by the Moghuls, are pictured in the background. The fort, which enclosed palaces, halls, and gardens, embodies the storied history of the Punjab capital, which has been ruled by Hindus, Muslims, Sikhs, and the British. The Badshahi Mosque, a Moghul monument made from marble and sandstone, which stands opposite the fort gate, is prominently painted. The Minar-a-Pakistan, the tower that commemorates the country's independence, is also captured in the painting. This portrait of Lahore—the "heart of Pakistan," Tariq calls it—is an important touchstone for customers.

A "family" restaurant, as the owners describe it, Ravi Kabob is popular with Pakistani clans from Arlington, Sterling, Springfield, and other northern Virginia suburbs. Other customers come for spicy barbecue from as far away as Pennsylvania. Extended families, often representing several generations, cluster around tables packed together. Fathers, who might be engineers or systems analysts, dress in crisp plaid shirts and Dockers. Wives and grandmothers are likely to wear traditional clothing. Young children in American-style T-shirts prance around the restaurant, and baby carriages are common.

The Pakistani community is maturing. Single men have called for their families to join them. Even some taxi drivers, the bread-and-butter clientele of the Pakistani café, are now accompanied by wives and children. Even as they put down roots, customers also keep their ties to home: A flyer on the door advertises the services of Khyber Money Transfer.

Other nationalities wander in to sample the food. Two Sudanese men, who lack their own ethnic restaurant to patronize, are comforted by Ravi's *halal* cooking. A Jordanian diner finds parallels between his country's dishes and Pakistan's. Vietnamese friends discover an unfamiliar but pleasing food.

Ravi's kebab plates have the invigorating flavor of outdoor cooking, of meat fresh off the fire. Small chunks of chicken on the bone colored a vivid orangish-red are charred on the outside and tender and moist within. The spicy, juicy kebabs arrive with nan; barbecued meat and the thick, flat bread are inseparable in the kebab house. Diners wrap chicken in the nan or just tear off a crunchy piece of the blistered bread and savor the taste. Chutney is another essential in the kebab ritual; customers dip kebabs or bread in this yogurt sauce, which is tangy with fresh coriander.

Another kebab, the *seekh*, is shaped like a sausage. Garnished with coriander leaves, the roll of ground beef is perked up with ginger and green pepper. Bits of coriander leaves that have been kneaded into the meat lend their fragrance.

A *lassi,* a yogurt drink avidly consumed in the Punjab countryside, is a delightful foil to the kebabs. Its sweet creaminess contrasts with the charcoaled meaty flavor of chicken, lamb, and beef. In Lahore, Tariq points out, diners order large pitchers of *lassi* to fortify themselves with strength and energy.

Each of the tantalizingly named kebabs on Ravi's panoramic menu has its own story and lore. The *seekh,* Persian for "skewered meat," derives from the Turkish term *sis,* which variously means "rapier," "fencing foil," "skewer," or "spit." Turkish warriors, the story goes, threaded meat on their swords and used them as cooking instruments on the steppes.

Tikka kebabs are small morsels of skewered chicken or other meat. Like *seekh, tikka* ("small pieces") derives from the Persian. The *shami* kebab, a beef patty filled with yellow split peas, is cooked in a frying pan. The *shami,* which means "early evening" in Persian, Mohammed explains, is a late afternoon snack.

The *chapli* kebab, a delicacy along the border frontier between Pakistan and Afghanistan, gets its name from the resemblance of the pungent burger to a sandal, or *chapal,* a word from Dari, an Afghani language similar to Persian. Ravi's cooks enhance the *chapli* with crushed red pepper, dried pomegranate seeds, and spring onions.

☆ ☆

What of the genesis of the kebab itself? Is it uniquely Pakistani, or did it come from elsewhere? The answer is a mixture of myth and history. Mohammed Afzal insists that the credit goes to the Turks, who spread their cooking technique to every land they conquered. Tariq traces the kebab to the "frontier," particularly to the city of Peshawar in Pakistan's Northwest Frontier province.

Both explanations have germs of truth. The Moghul Turks, who dominated what would become the northwest regions of Pakistan and India, brought with them a tradition of outdoor cooking. The warriors slaughtered lamb and sheep and avidly barbecued it. Turkish herdsmen, some speculate, also began making yogurt in order to carry milk over long distances. Yogurt (a Turkish word) was also absorbed into Indian and Pakistani cooking.

The Turks borrowed the word "kebab" from the Persians, the source of so much of the South Asian cooking lexicon. The Persians, like the Arabs, referred to any cooked meat as a kebab. The name may have been Persian, but the Turks possessed the technique long before they appropriated the word. The Moghuls and later tribesmen developed a repertoire of skewered meat dishes prepared in a lavish manner.

The warriors, argues food historian Ayla Algar, also introduced tandoor baking to the subcontinent. "Tandoor" is a word for the clay oven the Turkish tribes carried on their treks to bake the long, flat bread known throughout Central Asia as nan. Tandoori bread provided an exciting alternative to common griddle bread, such as *chapatis*.

The Moghuls, like so many invaders before them, advanced through the Khyber Pass and then through the Punjab on their march into India. It was in this anarchic frontier region on the border between present-day Afghanistan and Pakistan where kebab cooking thrived. Hard-bitten, gun-toting Pathan tribesmen still roam the rugged territory. Their law rules, Tariq says, in a region that has no "government."

Nature on the Northwest Frontier is invigorating. "You drink the water and you feel hungry again," says Tariq, who has relatives in the region. The Pathans, the local tribesmen who have learned to live off the land, are voracious meat eaters. "The slaughter of animals and the eating of flesh corresponds to a basic code of manliness" in this culture, writer Stephen Alter maintains. "Meat is seen as an essential part of the diet for it gives a man strength and vitality."

Open-air cooking was a technique the Pathans shared with the Moghuls. Kebabs were a natural meal in the raw environment. Simple spicing, with heavy use of black pepper and other basic seasonings, was the rule. The lawless frontier probably contributed the unadorned kebab to Pakistani cooking.

Ravi Kabob's *chapli* kebab is a specialty of Peshawar, the Pakistani trading city at the foot of the Khyber Pass. In this "frontier town" (the translation of its name), kebabs are a fixture of the bazaar. Shoppers, who hunt for apricots, almonds, and walnuts and sip Chinese green tea, smell the smoky fragrance of kebabs that vendors are cooking over charcoal grills.

☆ ☆

Ravi's proprietors treat kebab cooking as a craft. "Cooking is a big art," says Tariq, who has channeled his aesthetic sensibilities into the kitchen. Different kebabs demand different coloring: Chicken on the bone has a bright reddish-orange color; boneless chicken has a yellowish tinge. Food must "look good and taste good," Tariq says. No ordinary commodity, the kebab also requires the skillful blending of ginger, black pepper, coriander, garlic, and other spices. Ravi cooks prepare their kebabs over charcoal to produce a robust, outdoor flavor. Unlike many Indian restaurants, where the tandoor reigns, this Virginia eatery reserves the clay oven for baking bread.

Ravi also serves other traditional Pakistani dishes. The most famous is the *karahi*, named for the woklike pan in which it is cooked. The tomatoey stews of lamb or chicken are sprinkled with coriander and made fragrant with slivers of ginger. *Karahi* is another frontier food, often associated with Landi Kotal, a smuggling outpost in Pakistan at the highest point of the Khyber Pass. Traditionally, the stew was simmered over an open fire and eaten directly from the pan. In a concession to modern tastes, the restaurant serves the stew on paper plates.

On the weekend, Ravi prepares other rib-sticking classics. *Haleem* is a spicy mixture of beef, rice, lentils, and wheat. *Nehari* (Urdu for "morning"), a spicy beef-shank curry, was traditionally eaten in the morning by Pakistani workmen to stoke their stomachs.

Tariq and Mohammed want Ravi Kabob to be known above all else for its "Punjabi home cooking." The Punjabis, who live in their country's breadbasket, are enthusiastic about earthy, country food. Lentils and chickpeas are passions. Yellow split peas, slowly cooked to a delectable tenderness, and chickpeas (*chole*), steeped in a rich gravy, are regulars on the Ravi steam table. Chicken cooked with chickpeas, a Lahore dish, is a weekday special. A Ravi curry that combines chickpea flour and yogurt is another spicy Punjabi standard.

When the staff breaks for lunch, they explain the kebab phenomenon to a visitor by using analogies from American merchandising. Different styles of barbecue in Pakistan, they say, are associated with different towns and regions. Each variety has its own loyalists. *Peshawari* kebab, manager Syed Siraj Din points out, is like Chicago pizza. Can brand-name kebabs in America be far behind?

Ravi's proprietors relish the thought of kebabs being as popular as pizza, hamburgers, and hot dogs. The kebab is fast becoming an "international" food, Tariq says. There is no contest, brother Mohammed insists, between the kebab and American fast food. His product is already "fresher and cheaper."

Business is not all-consuming at Ravi Kabob House. Respectful of its clients' customs and traditions, the restaurant offers a quiet oasis during the Ramadan season. As dusk approaches, Tariq lays out *pakoras* (vegetable fritters) and dates to break the fast. A pitcher of *rooh afza*, a traditional Pakistani Ramadan refreshment made with milk and rose water, stands on the counter.

Unlike earlier Muslim food makers, the restaurateurs make no attempt to disguise their identity. They are no less assertive about their cuisine. No imitations of "Indian food" will suffice at Ravi Kabob House.

CHAPTER 7

Papaya and Plantain: Latin Cooking in America

Chili Weather: Southwestern Food Moves North

"MARTHA HAS RAVEN HAIR and sparkling eyes with a smile and toss of the head that makes you think of Carmen. She is out in all her glory and peacock feathers tonight." Martha, pictured by Texas writer Frank Bushick, was one of the "chili queens," who hosted the chili stands in San Antonio's Military Plaza during the 1890s. At dusk, pots of chili were wheeled in wagons to the square. The gaily dressed ladies served up pungent chili con carne brewing in cauldrons heated over mesquite or charcoal fires. Aromas of oregano and cumin wafted over the grounds. They also sold tortillas, tamales, coffee, and cinnamon-scented *atole*, a popular Mexican drink. The price for chili, a side of frijoles (beans), and a tortilla—a dime.

The women, commonly of Mexican background, smiled, joked, flirted, and bantered with customers and passersby. Luminous from the cooking fires and the red, yellow, and orange lanterns that swung over the dining patches, they beckoned to strollers in the plaza. Chili eaters sat on benches around wobbly tables covered by oil skins with checkerboard patterns. Musicians serenaded them with songs. The festivities brought together a varied assortment of diners. "A Mexican bootblack and a silk-hatted tourist would line up and eat side by side,"

Bushick wrote. "Cowboys, merchants, and hack drivers touched elbows. It was the genuine democracy of Bohemia."

The Plaza Mercado, known for its closely guarded presidio, jail, and drill grounds, where prisoners were executed, now had the bustle of a "veritable midway," observed San Antonio historian Donald Everett. "Mustangs, mules, donkeys, ox teams, wagons, lumber, hides, cotton, whites, blacks, half breeds . . . and Mexicans" jammed the market, one visitor reported. In addition to the chili queens, the plaza drew scores of vendors. Mexicans traded chili peppers, and hawkers showed off their songbirds—mockingbirds and cardinals—in wicker cages.

The vibrancy attracted writers who romanticized the plaza. Martha, the chili queen, wooed Stephen Crane with her charms and her wares. She plucked a rose from her corsage and pinned it to his jacket.

O. Henry, who frequently traveled to San Antonio from Austin, was entranced by the plaza spectacle of "travelers, rancheros, family parties, gay gasconading rounders, sightseers and prowlers of the polyglot." In the short story "The Enchanted Kiss," he warmed to the "delectable meats minced with aromatic herbs and poignant chile colorado" of the chili stands.

Churches, plazas, presidios, and fiestas gave this former Spanish mission town a Latin flavor. "The sauntering Mexicans prevail on the pavements," Frederick Law Olmsted recalls. The Laredito, San Antonio's Mexican quarter, was a demimonde of saloons, honky-tonks, and crowded dwellings. Anglos in search of the exotic visited cottages that had been converted into makeshift eateries.

In a *Scribner's* article in 1894, Edward King recounted a visit to one such "hovel": "The fat, swarthy Mexican mater-familias will place before you savory compounds, swimming in fiery pepper, which biteth like a serpent; and the tortilla, a smoking hot cake, thin as a shaving and about as eatable, is the substitute for bread. This meal, with bitterest of coffee to wash it down . . . , will be an event in your gastronomic experience."

The chili dispensed on the plaza had an unmistakable Mexican taste. The street-market dish, a variation on *chili colorado* (red chili), was an unadorned stew made from cheap cuts of meat covered with a blazing sauce. It was akin to an inexpensive and filling meal enjoyed by poor Mexican families. "When they have to pay for meat in the market a very little is made to suffice a family; it is generally cut into a kind of hash with nearly as many peppers as there are pieces of meat," observed J. C. Clopper, an early Texas colonist, in 1828 after a visit to San Antonio.

Chili, a popular story suggests, came to Texas with the washer-women who accompanied the Mexican armies during the period 1830–1840. When the soldiers retreated, the *lavanderas* went to work for the American militia. During the day, they boiled the clothes in large iron pots, which they converted to chili cooking at night. The stew might be beef, deer, or goat, livened up with red pepper and oregano.

Others trace this often written- and puzzled-about American dish to the rangelands of the Southwest. Ingenious chuck-wagon cooks, called "campuks," it is said, concocted the stew for hungry cowboys on trail drives. They simmered beef or buffalo, sometimes armadillo or jackrabbit, which they flavored with cumin, chili pepper, garlic, and onions picked on the trail. The chilies were tiny wild berries that turned from green to cherry red. These "little scorchers, the size of buck shot," writer Joe E. Cooper called them, were loved by wolves, coyotes, and, of course, birds. To keep a ready supply of spices, the cooks planted gardens of their spices in mesquite patches along their route.

☆ ☆

The dish called chili took its name from the tantalizing New World plant of ancient lineage. Chili, scholar Jean Andrews points out, was born in South America and migrated to the Caribbean and Mexico. European mariners found the tantalizing pods on the island of Hispaniola (home today to Haiti and the Dominican Republic), where they were a staple of the Carib Indians' diet. The Caribs called them *axi*—changed to *aji* by the Spaniards—and used them to enliven their bland diet of cassava, maize, beans, and fish. The islanders endured winters in the mountains "with the aid of the meat they eat with very hot spices," Columbus reported. The curious chilies, the Spaniards discovered, scorched the skin. The Indians bombarded the garrison that Columbus left in Hispaniola with gourds filled with ashes and ground pepper.

In pursuit of a direct route to the Indies and its rich supplies of black pepper, the explorers assumed the pungent fruits were "peppers," a name that has been linked to chilies ever since. They were probably Scotch bonnet peppers, plump, orange chilies named for their resemblance to the hat.

The Spanish carried chili seeds back from the Caribbean to the mother country. By the early 1500s, chili plants were springing up in Spain's gardens. They dubbed the spice "pimento" after their word *pimienta*, for black pepper.

Mexico had a vaster storehouse of chilies. When the conquerors invaded, they discovered a crop that the Indians had been cultivating for thousands of years, perhaps even before corn. Archaeological evidence, geographer Carl Sauer points out, suggests that the spice was being grown before 3500 B.C.

"The chili seller . . . sells mild red chiles, broad red chiles, hot green chiles, yellow chiles. He sells water chiles . . . smoked chiles, thin chiles, those like beetles. He sells hot chiles, the hollow-based kind. He sells green chiles, sharp pointed red chiles." As Spanish friar Bernardino de Sahagun reported in 1569, Aztec folkways were steeped in chili. The Spanish borrowed the Indians' name for the plant, *chilli*, and changed its spelling to chili.

Radiated by the sun, bushes of red, scarlet, orange, and yellow fruits grew in Indian plots. Strings of peppers dried on adobe walls. Chilies were smoked, roasted, pickled, or eaten raw. Lacking salt, the tribes sparked simple dishes of beans or maize with chilies, sometimes with additions of tomatoes. The chilies fired up the appetite and aided digestion of starchy foods.

The Aztecs were attuned to the varied flavors and temperatures different chilies produced. They divided chilies according to the heat they emitted: "very, very hot," "brilliant hot," "runaway hot," and so on. The different properties determined how each was best employed or blended in cooking.

Chilies were a critical ingredient in the *mollis*, the stews prepared for Indian royalty. "The lords also ate many kinds of casseroles . . . one kind . . . of fowl made . . . with red chile and tomatoes, and ground squash seeds . . . ; they ate another casserole of fowl made with yellow chile," Friar Sahagun wrote. The most celebrated dish, *mole poblano*, was typically turkey suffused in a sauce of chili paste, mixed with chocolate, cinnamon, raisins, and other aromatic flavorings.

Chilies were powerful cultural symbols. Signs of wealth, baskets of pods were sent as tribute by subjects to their kings. They were sacraments that were renounced during fasts. The chili also represented male potency, sometimes the phallus itself. A pepper with its seeds removed was considered "caponized," or emasculated.

The spice was both revered and feared. Disobedient children, servants, and wives were suspended over fires of chili. The Mayans punished young girls who looked at men by rubbing pepper in their eyes.

Chili was also a popular health remedy. The Indians took pepper mixes to alleviate sore throats, ear infections, and coughs. The Mayans treated infected gums by holding peppers in their mouths. The Aztecs rubbed mashed chilies into aching bones and muscles. The Spaniards came to believe in the chili's medicinal powers, and some in the seventeenth century began eating two roasted peppers after each meal to improve their vision. Sailors carried pickled peppers, a rich source of vitamin C, on their voyages to prevent scurvy.

Europeans marveled at the colorful plant. Writing in 1597, John Gerard, an English apothecary, was transfixed as he observed a flowering chili. "The flowers groweth along the stalks out of the wings of the leaves. After them groweth the cods, greene at first and when they be ripe of a brave colour, glittering like red corall, and of a hot, biting taste." Others were apprehensive. Jose de Acosta, a sixteenth-century Jesuit priest, was worried that consuming too much chili, an Indian aphrodisiac, would lead to sensual excess: "[I]t is very hote, fuming and pierceth greatly so as the use thereof is prejudicial to the health of young folkes, chiefly to the soule, for that it provokes to lust."

☆ ☆

In the mid-nineteenth-century Southwest, chili's appeal was limited to Mexicans and daring Anglos. An improbable figure, German café owner William Gebhardt, took it from the margins to a wider audience. Gebhardt, who settled during the 1840s in New Braunfels, a town near San Antonio, arrived as part of a large German immigrant wave that brought beer gardens to the riverbanks of the area. He opened a café in the back of a saloon in 1892. After sampling Mexican food in San Antonio, he bought a wagonload of peppers from Mexico and began making chili. His German clientele soon became devotees of the dish.

Gebhardt faced a serious obstacle—chili in Texas was seasonal, dependent on the spring pepper harvest. Determined to offer it year-round, he started experimenting. The avid tinkerer dried peppers in his mother-in-law's oven and ran bits of chili through a small meat grinder. He blended the resulting powder with oregano, cumin, and garlic and stored it in airtight bottles.

He set up a factory in San Antonio to manufacture the spice he affectionately called "Tampico dust" (after a Mexican town). In the early days, the plant turned out five cases of powder a week, which Gebhardt carried in a wagon and peddled throughout the city. The celebrated "powder man" kept improving his production methods, ultimately inventing thirty-seven machines for the factory.

Meanwhile, other chili promoters were trying to boost the spice's reputation. Dewitt Clinton Pendery launched the Mexican Chili Supply Company in 1890, which marketed chili pods and peppers. His company, which would develop a mail-order business, extolled the chili as an elixir: "[D]ishes such as chili con carne . . . act as a tonic upon the system. . . . The health-giving properties of hot chili peppers have no equal. They give tone to the alimentary canal, regulating the natural functions, giving a natural appetite and promoting health by action on the kidneys, skin, and lymphatics."

Gebhardt sold his Mexican Food Company in 1911 to his brothers-in-law, who added cans of chili con carne and tamales to its line. San Antonio boosters cheered the success of the enterprise and its most famous item. "It is the only product of its kind having that real Mexican tang," one publication said.

The company, which became the world's largest importer of Mexican spices, enticed housewives to buy chili powder. A 1923 ad promoted the Eagle Brand as a "delightful seasoning for all kinds of meats, fish, soups, salads, and salad dressings, but healthful in every way." A cookbook published by the company to "capture the glamour and romance of old Mexico" popularized chili-based recipes.

More shrewd marketing followed. The company offered shoppers in 1924 a "Mexican dinner package," which assembled one can of chili con carne, one can of "Mexican-style" beans, one can of shuck-wrapped tamales, two cans of Deviled Chili Meat, and one bottle of chili powder.

By the early 1900s, chili cooking was departing San Antonio's open-air markets for a new home, the chili parlor. The heyday of the chili queens was over. The cafés offered basic food in a spare setting. Cooks, who had often run chuck-wagon kitchens, prepared their grub in kitchens hidden behind blankets. At the counter, customers consumed bowls of "Texas red," the traditional chili-laced beef stew, or a bowl of "medium," with a side of pinto beans, a staple of cooking out on the range and standard fare on the ranches. Except for soda crackers and coffee, there was little to accompany the dish. As the chili joints built a following, Saturday-night excursions to the eateries became a popular pastime.

Texas red got its name from its red chili color, not from tomatoes. Chili purists, then and now, insist that the tomato defiles the true Texas dish. "Adding tomato to a pint of chili is like gouging too deeply with a diaper pin," chili aficionado Joe E. Cooper insists.

☆ ☆

Chili and other Tex-Mex products soon migrated north. The Chicago World's Fair in 1893 introduced visitors to Southwestern food at the San Antonio Chili Stand. In the early 1900s, Chicago's downtown workers bought chicken tamales from street vendors. Armour's and Libby, McNeill & Libby canned chili con carne and tamales in their Chicago plants.

Chili caught fire in the Midwest, where the most popular variety was "chili mac," a relatively bland garlic-free dish served in taverns, diners, and cafés that was a mélange of meat sauce, peppers, tomatoes, and elbow macaroni. John Isaac, the son of a Lithuanian miner who had emigrated to Pennsylvania, was a Midwestern chili pioneer. Isaac ran a saloon in Aurora, Illinois, offering a drawing card of a free chicken lunch. When the town voted to ban liquor in 1912, the entrepreneur moved to Green Bay, Wisconsin, where he opened a diner. Isaac expanded on the chili mac by creating a layered dish of pasta, beans, and meat sauce. According to legend, he also conceived the oyster cracker. Dissatisfied with the soda cracker for chili dipping, Isaac, who also sold oysters in season, persuaded a biscuit company to manufacture a smaller item.

Immigrant entrepreneurs in Cincinnati produced more chili incarnations. Tom Keradjieff, a Macedonian who emigrated with other peasant villagers from the Balkans in the early twentieth century, learned the hot-dog business by working at "coney island" stands in New York City. The vendors named their product after the Brooklyn seaside resort, where early purveyors of hot dogs, like Nathan's Famous, operated.

Keradjieff moved to Cincinnati, where many of his countrymen worked in the railyards. He found a shop next to the Empress Theatre in 1923 and opened a coney island business. In search of a tempting chili sauce for his franks, he concocted a spice mix that combined cinnamon, allspice, cloves, nutmeg, chili, and other flavorings.

Keradjieff had a brainstorm: He would not only ladle his sauce on hot dogs but also serve it with spaghetti. The Empress, as he called the establishment, began by selling separate plates of chili and pasta. His customers soon began mixing the two together, and some of them suggested that Keradjieff put the chili directly on top of the pasta.

He introduced this twist in the 1930s and invented more toppings—cheese, onions, beans. Patrons now could choose among a bowl of plain chili; a "two way," chili over spaghetti; a "three way," chili spaghetti topped with cheddar cheese; and a "four way," chili spaghetti with layers of cheese and onions. The pièce de résistance, a "five way," featured the pungent chili spaghetti with successive layers of kidney beans, onions, and cheddar cheese.

Macedonian and Greek businessmen copied the Empress formula. Nick Sarakatsannis, the founder of the Dixie Chili chain, praised the commercial genius of Keradjieff, a man he called "an Edison, a Firestone":

> Everybody, in the old days in the regular restaurants, they had roast beef, roast pork, roast lamb. . . . So next day they scrape up all that meat, they grind it and they make chili. They put beans in it, and they call it chili con carne. But in 1923 the Empress, they buy freshly ground beef and they cook it. No roast pork or roast beef or leftovers. They use pure beef, no beans. The idea was to have plain meat chili to prove it wasn't leftovers. And they add the spaghetti. From then on, we all copied. I had my own chili, but I copied the spaghetti.

Keradjieff's tiny shop, Sarakatsannis observed, pulled in customers: "The customers on Vine Street, they pass by the place and they smell it and they walk in. It was just a small, tight place—it could seat maybe fifteen, twenty people, but they did good business. It is such a beautiful dish. But it was the price that drew them, too.

Coney island five cents. Chili spaghetti fifteen cents. With cheese it was twenty-five cents."

After World War II, the early shops spawned chains. Immigrant clans built strings of parlors with names like Goldstar, Skyline, and Acropolis, which provided job opportunities to family and newly arrived kin. Central kitchens began turning out chili, which was trucked to shops where it was dispensed from steam tables. The server took the customer's plate and assembled the necessary combination from the line of crocks filled with onions, cheese, and other fixings.

Cincinnati chili, folklorist Timothy Lloyd pointed out, had a Balkan accent. The spicing, common to Greece, Macedonia, and other parts of the region, emphasized cinnamon, allspice, cloves, and nutmeg, whose sweetness was a foil to sharper flavors like chili, garlic, and cumin. Chili peppers also were not uncommon in Macedonian recipes. Chili must have reminded Keradjieff of casseroles like moussaka and *pastitsio* (a Balkan macaroni), which were often made with a sauce of ground beef and tomato. He took a Southwestern classic and imbued it with the fragrance of his homeland.

☆ ☆

Coney island shops, usually Greek-owned businesses selling chili-drenched hot dogs, were springing up throughout the country. In the early 1900s, young Greek immigrants Peter Curtis and Anthony Antonakos traveled from New York to Johnstown, Pennsylvania, to work as apprentices in a candy shop owned by a countryman. They opened their own candy and ice cream business in Cumberland, Maryland, in 1905.

A Greek peddler from Texas visited their shop and planted a profitable idea. Alexis, the only name he was known by in family history, appeared with a "little burner on his back," Louis Giatras, the owner of the business today, said. "He had a special sauce they could make money with." The itinerant Greek cooked up samples of his chili sauce over the burner; the partners loved it. They took the recipe and started selling coney island hot dogs. The restaurant, originally named the coney island Lunch and now known as the Coney Island Famous Wiener Company, is still thriving.

Paterson, New Jersey, became a bastion of the "hot Texas wiener," another variation on the coney. Its originator, an anonymous elderly Greek, owned a lunch counter in downtown Paterson in the 1920s. Looking for ways to spice up his hot dogs, he dabbled with different chili mixes. His favorite, folklorist Timothy Lloyd points out, resembled a "Greek spaghetti sauce." Similar to the Cincinnati chili flavoring, it played chili and cumin off against cinnamon and allspice.

A product was born that a long line of Greek-owned lunchrooms in this industrial town would merchandise. Their stock-in-trade, the hot Texas wiener, was fried, put in a steamed bun, and then topped with successive layers of mustard, chopped onions, and chili sauce. The "grills," as they were known in Paterson lingo, also sold hamburgers, BLTs, and roast beef sandwiches.

New grills sprang up from the old. Employees moved on to open their own businesses. William Pappas, who had worked at the original Texas wiener business, started Libby's Hot Grill. Libby's, in turn, became a launching pad for more eateries. The Falls View, the Olympic, and other successors located near the textile mills that hugged the Passaic River offered cheap and filling meals to the area's factory workers.

Greeks in Providence, Rhode Island, also put their own unmistakable stamp on the frankfurter. In the 1940s, Greek vendors in Providence, according to food writer Paul Lukas, popularized a griddle-cooked hot dog smothered in a sauce that resembled chili. To highlight its heritage, they called their style the "New York System." They named their shops, which expanded around the state, in the same unconventional way—for example, Sam's New York System Restaurant.

The immigrants made Detroit the capital of coney island chili. Constantine "Gust" Keros, a Greek, started out in Detroit sweeping floors at the Kelsey Hayes auto plant in 1910 and then drove a pop-corn wagon. His brother, William, recently arrived from Greece, became Gust's partner in 1914 in a new venture, the American Hat Cleaning and Shoe Shine Parlor. Three years later, the restless businessmen launched the American Coney Island, a storefront eatery, in downtown Detroit. They sold nickel hot dogs slathered with chili to factory workers. William later left to launch his own restaurant, Lafayette Chili, which was next door to his brother's shop and offered the same menu.

The brothers were devoted to their adopted land. They called their hot dogs "coney islands," Gust's son, Chuck, recalled, because "it was so American, I think. And that was their whole life." For all their patriotism, they could not resist giving their product an ethnic touch. In addition to the smell of mustard and onions, their hot dogs, like hot Texas wieners, were fragrant with a cinnamon and allspice chili sauce.

Coney shops have spread from downtown Detroit in recent years to new neighborhoods, malls, and shopping centers and expanded to other Michigan towns. "Now there's one on every corner," Tony Keros, William Keros's son, told the *Detroit News*. The businesses burgeoned by tapping a large supply of family members from the "other side." After learning the craft, many embarked on their own coney businesses. Twenty of Chuck Keros's cousins, who emigrated from Greece, operate coney shops today.

Even in the heartland of chili, the Southwest, the product has metamorphosed. James Coney Island Company, a twenty-four-shop franchise headquartered in Houston, grew out of a chili café started by two Greek immigrants, Tom and James Papadakis, in 1923. They sold chili by the bowl as well as in pint- and quart-size containers. Customers also could buy frozen one-pound bricks of chili to go.

The brothers, who had disembarked at Ellis Island, sampled coney island hot dogs in New York City. They made the chili-laden frank the centerpiece of their business. James's repertoire now includes New York– and Chicago–style hot dogs, jalapeño dogs, Polish sausage, and "fit franks," a low-fat choice.

Moros y Cristianos: The Goya Food Empire

The Goya delivery truck was parked in front of the makeshift outdoor café at Manna, a Dominican eatery in Silver Spring, Maryland, an inner suburb of Washington, D.C. A pocket of Latin commerce filled a small strip on a rustic, woodsy street of small apartments and multi-family homes. Besides Manna, a record-video store that also sold moneygrams, a Hispanic barbershop, and a Peruvian restaurant marketed their services to the neighborhood's ethnics.

Inside Manna, a small television set broadcast a Spanish talk show, whose scantily clad female guests kept the young male customers riveted to the screen. A jukebox pulsed with merengue music and other Latin pop tunes. At a nearby table, an Ecuadoran peddler enticed customers with his pile of CDs featuring the latest Caribbean bands and Hispanic heartthrobs. In rapid-fire, voluble patrons bantered and joked with the restaurant staff working behind the counter. Menacing masks with horns, a drum, and other Dominican artifacts as well as photographs of the country's American baseball idols adorned the wall.

The earthy menu of seafood soup, yuca (cassava), plantains and *tostones* (fried green plantains), avocado salad, and hearty stews draws a steady flow of diners. Shrimp a la Manna, a house specialty, arrives in a tangy, long-simmered sauce of tomatoes, olives, bits of green onions, capers, crunchy green peppers, and coriander. A huge platter of white rice and a coffee cup of red beans round out the feast. For an extra spark, there is Manna's orange-colored hot sauce, spiked with chili and redolent of citrus and vinegar.

Sacks of Canella rice are stacked against the wall of the tiny dining room. Canella, a Goya brand name for a long-grain rice, is slang for a young, skinny leg. Cresencia Torres, or "Manna" as she likes to be called, prefers this product because "the rice is not cut." She also buys roman cranberry beans, another mainstay of her menu, from Goya. They are a particular favorite even though they are not the same beans she cooked with in the Dominican Republic. "We use this one because they are creamy."

Packs of Goya soft drinks are stacked on the floor. The restaurant orders amber cans of Malta, a sugar-laden malt beverage beloved in Puerto Rico and the Dominican Republic. A German company in the Dominican Republic manufactured a similar drink from brown sugar-cane, and fans there mixed it with sweetened condensed milk. "They think it makes you strong," Manna says.

Goya also sells her cola champagne, a bubbly soda popular with Salvadorans and other Central Americans. Cans of pear juice, mango, guava, pineapple, coconut, and other tropical drinks are delivered regularly by the company. Manna, who also makes such tropical-fruit drinks as papaya, passion fruit, and *morir sonando* (die dreaming), a blend of milk and orange juice, is particularly fond of *mammee*. She buys it "fresh-frozen" from Goya and makes it into a pinkish drink, whose subtle sweetness is accented by cinnamon.

Sometimes known as the Santo Domingo apricot, *mammee* got its name from the Taino Indians, who made a wine from the brown-skinned fruit. It fascinated the Spanish writer Gonzalo Hernandez de Oviedo: "There is a fruit called mammee which grows on a large tree with beautiful cool leaves. The fruit is handsome . . . , of a very delicate flavor and its thickest part the size of two fists placed together." The pulp, he said, "tastes like peaches or even better, and is of very pleasant odor." Manna has fond memories of the fruits, which "looked like big avocados" and whose flesh resembled "red wine."

For restaurants like Manna, as well as supermarkets and bodegas, the Goya truck is a commercial lifeline linking them to the vast stocks of Latin and Caribbean products—more than a thousand—merchandised by America's largest Hispanic-owned company. Shipping delays, such as those that developed in the wake of 9/11, can be perilous for restaurants like Manna, which stopped receiving its regular supplies of beans after the disaster.

☆ ☆

The founder of the food giant Goya, Don Prudencio Unanue, was born in Burgos, a Basque region of northern Spain. The young adventurer moved to Puerto Rico in 1902 where the seventeen-year-old met his future bride, Doña Caroline Casal. In 1918, Don Prudencio left Puerto Rico for New York to begin studies at the Albany Business School. Four years later he was working as a clerk for a customs broker in New York. It may have been this experience that kindled his interest in the import business.

Unanue opened a small firm in 1928 to bring in products from his native Spain. The importer expected that Manhattan's large Spanish émigré community, centered in Chelsea, would be a prime market for his olives, olive oil, and sardines.

When Spain erupted in civil war, in the mid-1930s, Unanue's sources were cut off. He turned to Morocco and Tunisia, Mediterranean countries that grew similar products, to fill the gap. He bought a warehouse and began packing olives and olive oil at a plant in lower Manhattan.

At this precarious time, Prudencio received a godsend—a shipment of 500 cases of Moroccan sardines from a Spanish manufacturer. In 1936 he bought the product's brand name, Goya, from his benefactor for $1. The family business, Unanue and Sons, would adopt the Goya name in 1946.

An unexpected event, the large wave of Puerto Rican immigrants who arrived after World War II, changed the company's focus from Iberia to Puerto Rico, which Unanue had always considered his "second home." The Caribbeans were different from the Spaniards, who emigrated as individuals, observed Conrad Colon, the company's longtime vice president of marketing. They were "one of the first groups to migrate in masses."

Prudencio established a foothold in Puerto Rico, building the island's first packing plant. Goya not only would export from the island but also would sell to its people. "If we can sell to Puerto Ricans here, why not in Puerto Rico?" Rafael Toro, Goya's public relations chief, explained. Moreover, when the Caribbeans moved to the United States, they would look for products they already knew.

Peasants who had flocked to Puerto Rican cities during the 1940s began leaving for America as the economy deteriorated. Encouraged by cheap flights from San Juan to New York—less than $50 for a one-way ticket—the immigrants streamed into Kennedy airport with dreams of a better life. The Puerto Rican community mushroomed from a population of 70,000 in 1940 to 250,000 in 1950.

The newcomers nestled in East Harlem, a neighborhood in New York City's Upper East Side, where previous generations of immigrants had put down roots. Irish and Germans, who settled there in the mid-1900s, were succeeded by Italians. In the 1940s, when the exodus of Italians was almost complete, the Caribbeans began moving into its housing projects and its four- and five-story tenements.

The quarter was known as El Barrio, or the "neighborhood." In this Puerto Rican stronghold, shops catered to the tastes of the immigrants. *Carnicerias* (butcher shops) stocked chorizo, spicy sausage, and other pork products. Snack bars offering *comidas criollos* (creole food) sold *pastelitos*—turnovers stuffed with chopped meat, mashed plantains, raisins, capers, and olives—and *bacalaitos*—codfish fritters, traditional holiday fare—and other treats. They served *refrescos* like tamarind, a brownish drink with a flavor at once sweet and tart that is made from the pulp of the bean-shaped pods of a tropical evergreen tree.

The atmosphere of a Caribbean market was re-created in a covered shopping area that stretched for five blocks of Park Avenue under the Grand Central railroad bridge. La Marqueta, the first of New York City's public covered markets, was opened in 1936 during Mayor La-Guardia's administration. It was established to provide more comfortable and sanitary accommodations for the hundreds of pushcart operators who worked in the open-air markets. Formerly Irish, Italian, and Jewish, the market now teemed with Hispanics who jostled among the food stalls, eating stands, fish stores, produce shops, and discount clothing vendors.

La Marqueta had all the qualities of a San Juan shopping district. "The radios roar mambos, merengues and rock, the customers haggle with vim and laughter, the vendors shout their bargains, the over-whelmed babies cry and color sparks off the fruit, the pink rayon skirts of the women and off the explosive hues of their headkerchiefs," writer Kate Simon observed. Caribbean produce was displayed, un-packaged and unwrapped, for customers to touch and fondle.

Long tubers with a scaly, barklike skin were piled in boxes. The yuca was the queen of the *viandas*, the root vegetables that had sus-tained Puerto Ricans since the time of slavery. The all-purpose starch, cultivated by the Taino Indians and adopted by the Africans, was a plentiful, durable plant as well as a source of high energy. It could be boiled, baked, roasted, fried, or grated into a flour or meal. The root was even used to make starch for clothes.

Heaps of green bananas were displayed in the market stalls. The immigrants called them *guineos*, a reference to the West African coun-try known for its banana groves. The Puerto Ricans fried them twice to make *tostones*, starchy banana slices—our "french fries," author Yvonne Ortiz called them. Baked, mashed, mixed with pork crack-lings, and seasoned with garlic, the plantain was transformed into *mo-fongo*, an island delicacy. A dish whose very name evoked Africa began as a breakfast food given to slaves on the sugar plantations.

La Marqueta was the place to hunt for unusual ingredients that were vital to the Puerto Rican kitchen. Shoppers snatched up *culantro*, a more intense variety of cilantro, and other herbs. Some stands car-ried *mauby* bark, from which the Tainos had made a cooling astringent drink. *Mauby* was a favorite *refresco* of the immigrants.

Prudencio Unanue stepped in to satisfy the islanders' basic wants. "We had the products that reminded them of home," his son, Joseph Unanue, recalled. Into La Marqueta the business carted 100-pound bags of rice and beans; customers scooped up as much as they wanted to buy.

The young business sold the dealers pigeon peas, a legume that the island's slaves had cultivated. Known variously as *congo*, *gungo*, *gunga*, and, in Spanish, *gandules*, the green field pea that grew on a hardy shrub originated in the Middle East. (Its seeds were uncovered in an

Egyptian tomb.) The pigeon pea was transplanted to West Africa and ultimately traveled to the Americas with the slave trade.

Taken green from the pod or dried to a brownish color with rusty speckles, the pea was regarded with special affection. Woven into rice, *gandules* were central to the island's national dish, *arroz con gandules*. At Christmas the plate was served with roast pork and *pasteles* (steamed meat patties).

The bodega, the corner store that the Puerto Ricans brought to America, was Goya's entrée to the immigrant market, first in East Harlem and later in the Bronx and Brooklyn. The company supplied the bodegas with a wide array of goods—rice and beans; boxes of dried codfish (a food that Puerto Rico acquired a taste for during slavery); amber bottles of guava, coconut, and tamarind syrups to make tropical drinks; and glass jars of black pepper, cumin, sesame seeds, and other spices. Goya also sold cans of *pasteles* and *mondongo* (tripe soup), papaya and guava preserves, chorizos, anchovies, and sardines.

The new firm cultivated the bodegas. "In the 1950s we sold only to bodegas. The bodega created us," Joseph Unanue pointed out. More than stores, they were community centers or social clubs with a fervent neighborhood following. Created as wine cellars or taverns in Spain, the shops in America sold Caribbean newspapers and circulated homeland gossip. They were gathering places where "people would go to find out what was happening in the community," Goya executive Toro remembers. Owners sometimes set up tables outside their bodegas for locals to play dominoes. The proprietor, in turn, became a trusted community figure. "Over here we know the history of most of our customers. The problems they have. We get invited to all the weddings and get invited to all the baptisms," a Boston bodega owner commented.

The owners, or *bodegeros*, offered immigrants modest but vital assistance. They provided credit, cashed checks, contributed to burial expenses, and translated documents. The tiniest purchase was welcome; customers could buy a single stamp or cigarette or a half loaf of bread. "People come to a bodega when they want something small and quick—that's our secret," said Albert Sabater, a store owner in East Harlem.

Goya salesmen called on bodegas to sell products as well as to gather intelligence about food trends. "Our salesmen talk daily to bodega owners to find out what their new customers want and we adjust our products to fit their needs," Conrad Colon noted. Goya strengthened its ties to the stores by offering them generous prices. Even when the supermarkets expanded in the 1960s, the company offered the bodegas the same terms as it did the chains. The practice continues today. "We protect them because they are our first customer," Colon added.

☆ ☆

Dominican immigration, which started as a small stream in the early 1960s and ballooned in the next two decades, boosted Goya's fortunes. The 500,000 Dominicans have become New York City's fastest-growing immigrant group. "Nuevo Yorko," as the immigrants call it, now has the world's largest Dominican community after Santo Domingo. Garment workers, cab drivers, cooks, and factory hands have expanded the company's customer base. "They are very loyal customers to our products," said Colon.

Goya looks to Dominicans both as customers and as canny retailers, who know not only their countrymen's tastes but also the buying habits of their other Latin clientele. They dominate the bodega business in New York City and own a majority of the independent supermarkets that operate in inner-city neighborhoods.

When Puerto Ricans wanted to sell their bodegas, the Dominicans lined up to buy them. The Puerto Ricans "started retiring and their kids were going into the professional world," Luis Salcedo, the Dominican-born director of the National Supermarket Association, said. In cities in Massachusetts, Rhode Island, Connecticut, and New Jersey, Dominicans were also taking over the bodegas from their predecessors. Wherever the entrepreneurs dispersed, the Goya marketers, always sharp observers of their clients' movements, sent salesmen in hot pursuit.

Dominican businessmen spotted an opening in the mid-1970s when supermarket chains closed their operations in poor New York City communities like the South Bronx and East Harlem. "They were aggressive to jump into an opportunity when a store closed," Luis Salcedo said of his fellow merchants. Wholesalers who were already supplying bodegas lent the Dominicans a hand. They enlisted promising *bodegeros* and helped them acquire the abandoned stores. Their sponsors provided advertising, sold them packaged goods, and assisted with financing. "They are very industrious," said Charles A. Krasne, president of Krasdale Foods, of the Dominicans. "And they stick their necks out. They came to New York to get rich and they succeeded."

Supermarket chains like C Town and Bravo, whose stores were mostly Dominican-owned, bloomed in New York's poor neighborhoods. Owners recruited relatives and friends to work in the businesses. After learning the fundamentals, some of the apprentices left to open their own stores. "It became a domino effect," Luis Salcedo commented.

The supermarkets' staples are "tropicals"—plantains, rice, beans, Latin fruit drinks—that are popular throughout the Caribbean. But owners, Salcedo points out, must be attuned to the unique palates of their clientele. "We study our communities and go out and get the products they like." Puerto Ricans, he learned, were enamored of the green plantain; Dominicans hankered for the ripe one. No "textbook businessman," he remembers discovering during his days as a retailer how fond his Dominican customers were of *batatas* (sweet potatoes). He ordered boxes shipped in so that they could make a traditional Good Friday dish.

Another wave of Latin immigrants, Cuban exiles, had swept into the United States in the late 1950s and early 1960s, expanding Goya's customer base. They built a colony in Miami, where Goya swiftly established a branch.

The second-largest settlement of the expatriates was concentrated in the Union City, New Jersey, area. The recently uprooted newcomers joined an older community of Cuban immigrants who had moved to this city across the Hudson from Manhattan in the 1940s to work in its embroidery factories and knitting mills. By 1981 the Cuban population in Union City and in West New York, the town next door, had grown to 100,000.

Union City Cubans considered Miami a sister city. Many traveled back and forth to visit relatives. Immigrants in Miami seeking better jobs looked for them in New Jersey. During the 1980s, a sign in Miami pointed north: "This way to Union City, New Jersey."

The newcomers created a vibrant commercial enclave along the ninety blocks of Bergenline Avenue, which ran from Union City into West New York. Like Calle Ocho, Miami's Cuban district, this Latin outpost boasted bakeries, butcher shops, grocery stores, and nightclubs. In their new home, Cubans carried on old customs. Patrons of *cantinas*, the traditional Cuban cafeterias, took their *cantinas* (aluminum pots) to these establishments to pick up a week's worth of food. They drank *café Cubano*, the stiff espresso, and refreshed themselves with *batidos*, milk shakes made from tropical fruits.

The neighborhood was fragrant with the smells of familiar dishes. Customers savored garlicky *lechon asado* (roast pork) and *ropa vieja* ("old rags"), a shredded-beef dish cooked in a tomato sauce that had originated as a handy way to use the meat from leftover roasts. The quintessential Cuban platter of rice and black beans revived memories of the homeland. Redolent of garlic, cumin, and lime, it was called *moros y cristianos*, an allusion to Iberia's Moorish invaders.

☆ ☆

The Puerto Ricans, Dominicans, and Cubans all shared common tastes. In their countries, "the basic thing is the olive oil, garlic, and oregano," Conrad Colon observed. Goya's merchants became keen students of the common threads and variations in their customers' diets.

Rice and beans anchor the meals of the Latin Caribbean. A staple of the Taino Indians, beans gradually became a basic foodstuff of the Afro-Caribbeans. During slavery in Puerto Rico, anthropologist Sidney Mintz points out, rice and beans, or *el matrimonio* (married couple), was a dish prepared on special occasions. It was offered in place of the normal fare of cornmeal or starchy root vegetables.

Puerto Ricans favored pink (*rosada*) and kidney (*marca diablo*) beans, while the Cubans lusted after black beans (*frijoles negros*). The Dominicans were enamored of the red roman or cranberry bean; their national dish of beans and rice was honored by naming it *la bandera*, for the country's red-and-white flag.

The islanders often had different names for the same product. Cubans call the papaya *fruta bomba* (like a grenade), while the Puerto Ricans refer to it as *lechosa* (milky). To the Dominicans, the orange is *china*; it is *naranja* to the Cuban.

Product labeling requires a sharp appreciation of the nuances of the food vocabulary. Goya has different labels for Cuban and Puerto Rican beans, *frijoles* and *habichuelas*, respectively. "If the Puerto Ricans call their beans *habichuelas*, we print the labels that go to Puerto Rican neighborhoods that way," Joseph Unanue, who succeeded his father as Goya president, revealed. "We want to make sure they find us right away."

Since the food of its Caribbean customers had a strong Spanish imprint, the company had a head start. Compared with Central American cooking, Cuban, Puerto Rican, and, to a lesser degree, Dominican food had stronger ties to the "mother country." In Mexico, for example, the Spanish conquerors were unable to destroy the indigenous culture. "The Spanish conquered Mexico, but they couldn't introduce their food," Colon observed. In the Caribbean, on the other hand, they decimated the Taino society.

Caribbean cooking is a creole blend, a medley of Spanish ingredients and tropical foodstuffs. By drawing on its large store of Spanish products and new Caribbean *sazons* (seasonings) and staples, Goya could supply the necessities for those hybrid dishes. An example is *asopao de pollo* (soupy chicken), a Puerto Rican classic. This dish, more like a thick chicken and rice stew, is a descendant, Raymond Sokolov suggests, of the soupy Spanish rice dishes, *arroces caldosos*, conceived in Valencia. When the Puerto Ricans immigrated to New York City, they continued to cook this festive dish. On Friday evenings in El Barrio, novelist Oswald Rivera remembers, the aromas of *asopao*, cooked by countless Puerto Rican mothers, permeated the tenements. "By the time most kids got home from school, the scent of peppercorns, chorizo and cured ham would fill the hallways and stairwells. . . . The strong, rich aroma of chicken stew would signal our time of solace."

The chicken is first seasoned with *adobo*, a fragrant mixture of onion, garlic, and oregano. The bird then is immersed in a sauce that combines Spanish élan with the lusty flavors of the Caribbean. *Recaito* ("daily shopping")—a medley of traditional cilantro with a spiny leaf variety found in Puerto Rico, sweet chili peppers (*aji dulces*), garlic, and other flavorings—provides its zest. Tomato sauce, a Spanish rendition made from a New World vegetable, is blended in. A mixture of olives, capers, and pimentos, roasted red peppers, peps up the sauce. This *alcaparrado*, a word of Arabic derivation, is a Spanish condiment that appeals to Caribbeans. It combines two tangy Mediterranean appetizers with a hors d'oeuvre the Spaniards created from the bell peppers they took from the Americas. They peeled and roasted the red peppers and then marinated them in olive oil.

The cooking oil itself has the aroma of ham, a Spanish inheritance, and the yellow-orange color of *achiote*, or *annatto*, a spice extracted from the dried seeds of a small bush widely grown in Latin America. *Achiote* is a plant with pink blossoms and soft spiny berries whose seeds are enclosed by an orange pulp. One of the oldest plants they cultivated, the Indians called the shrub "prickly plant seed." Puerto Rican cooks replaced saffron, the imperial spice and coloring agent the Arabs gave the Spanish, with a cheaper, homegrown ingredient.

Together, these flavorings constitute the *sofrito* (slowly fried), the cooking base for the stew. The islanders transformed the traditional cooking medium used by the Spanish—tomatoes, onions, and green peppers—into an earthier sauce.

Goya supplied the basic materials for the *asopao*. The cook could use the standard *adobo* in the yellow-capped jar, or the same seasoning with a lemon tang, that was aimed at Puerto Ricans. Most Latin stores stocked containers of Goya *sofrito*, as well as *achiote*, both in paste and powdered form. The company also sold the brilliant green *recaito* sauce. Goya products imported from Spain, including Valencia rice, olive oil, and *alcaparrado*, were indispensable for *asopao*.

☆ ☆

Now headquartered in Secaucus, New Jersey, Goya has been tirelessly modernizing its wares, packaging and preparing foods more efficiently, conveniently, and with flair. Beans and rice are no longer sold in bulk but in plastic packages, bags, and cans. Gone are the barrels and gunny sacks from which customers scooped Goya staples.

Packaged spice blends and flavorings have eased the burdens of the harried Latin homemaker. Seasoning a meal no longer requires the chopping, pounding, crushing, and blending traditional back home. Opening a spice packet or pouring a sauce, or *mojo*, from a bottle eliminates the need for the *pilon* and *maceta* (mortar and pestle).

Goya was making inroads in the supermarkets. In the Goya sections, a dazzling array of its thirty-four bean products and twenty-three rice items are displayed. Quick-serving dishes, like packaged rice and black beans, were early Latin convenience foods. Goya stocked grocery shelves with boxes of easy-to-prepare Mexican rice, yellow rice, and paella.

Goya products also became a fixture of the store freezer. For Cuban tastes, there was *ropa vieja*, a shredded-beef dish, and *arroz con pollo*, chicken and yellow rice. Dominicans and Puerto Ricans were offered rice and pigeon peas. *Pasteles*, originally sold in cans, now came in frozen packages. Even yuca, customarily purchased fresh, was now available on the freezer shelf.

The changes in wares mirrored changes in the Latin market. Goya's customers were a mixture of first-generation immigrants who adhered to food traditions and of younger ethnics as well as working women looking for cooking shortcuts. "Older Hispanics don't want prepared foods," said Mary Ann Unanue, a Goya executive and member of the founding family. "But the younger people don't have a problem with it. Young people are busy, they're used to the microwave, and they want to eat those things they grew up on that they don't have time to make or can't make as well as their mothers."

The old Latin neighborhoods were changing. Influxes of new Hispanic immigrants meant that Goya could no longer afford to focus exclusively on the Caribbean market. It was pressed to develop new products.

Salesmen were hearing strange food requests on their grocery calls. For example, in Miami's Little Havana during the mid-1980s, customers began asking for curious items the shops didn't carry. "The typical Cuban things weren't moving as well," Raul Diaz, a longtime Goya salesman, said. "All of a sudden, they were asking for flour to make *arepas*, red beans for *gallo pinto*. When the store owners start asking for things that are missing from the shelves, you go back and tell the company." The requests were coming from Nicaraguans, Hondurans, Colombians, and other Latins arriving in the neighborhood.

Another old Cuban stronghold, New Jersey's Union City–West New York area, was also acquiring a new complexion. As older Cuban residents retired and/or moved back to Miami in the early 1990s, South and Central American newcomers from Peru, Colombia, Ecuador, and Argentina took their place. Restaurants like Oh Que Bueno Ecuador that served up orange cornmeal griddle cakes, pepper fish soup with ground peanuts, and other specialties found an eager clientele on Bergenline Avenue.

In response to these trends, Goya sought to transform itself into a pan-Latin enterprise. For the Colombians, a rapidly growing group in the Northeast, Goya brought out *harina pan,* a corn flour they used to make *arepas,* the round corn cakes first fashioned by the Indians.

Filled with cheese, eggs, ham, and myriad other items, or taken plain, the Colombian bread was eaten at breakfast and other meals or as an all-day snack. For Peruvians, Goya imported the large purple olives they fancied. Bottles of *curtido*, a pickled cabbage salad, were marketed to Salvadorans, who served their *pupusas,* a variation on the tortilla, with the tangy condiment. After learning of the Salvadoran enthusiasm for Chinese food, Goya began selling the Central Americans chow mein.

The company was applying its time-honored marketing strategy. "Follow the trend of immigrating Hispanics who are coming in and market the products they know from home," Joseph Unanue said. Nevertheless, the company sometimes stumbled when introducing unfamiliar products. *Panela,* a brown sugar Colombians used for drinks and desserts, was first sold in granulated form. But consumers preferred to buy it in blocks, which they could scrape themselves; Goya accommodated them and manufactured a new item.

The largest Latin market, the Mexican community, was the hardest to break into. Mexican food, which relied heavily on chilies, corn, and beans, was more pungent than Caribbean cooking with its aromas of olive oil, garlic, and oregano. "There was difficulty in selling the same product to Mexican Americans. Most of our products are Caribbean in nature," Joseph Unanue remarked.

Mexican customers, moreover, were concentrated in the West and Southwest, while Goya's loyal base was in the Northeast. "We already had brand awareness in the Northeast," observed Rafael Toro. "We were going outside the Northeast where there's no brand awareness." Goya's early efforts to market its line of Mexican products failed because the ethnics were devoted to products they had regularly bought back home. "Immigrants have real loyalty to authentic Mexican brands," said Ignacia Hernandez, the president of a Mexico-based company that sold jalapeño peppers, mole sauces, and other items.

Goya was competing with well-entrenched products. Bimbo, a Mexican manufacturer, marketed tortillas, rolls, cakes, and cookies to shoppers who were already fans of its baked goods. Goya's tropical nectars were challenged by Mexico rival Jumex, whose tamarind, mango, and other drinks had an ardent following.

To compete more effectively, Goya forged partnerships with Mexican food companies. Goya now distributes La Ma Modena Pasta, made by the country's top pasta manufacturer. Mexican Americans are fond of soup made with vermicelli and enjoy macaroni, shells, and other noodles cooked with spicy tomato sauce.

With its long-established distribution network and well-known products, Goya was more successful selling to the new Mexican community in the Northeast. The Mexican population in New York City had surged, tripling in size during the 1990s to 187,000. The Puerto Rican population, on the other hand, declined more than 8 percent during the same period.

In New York City's El Barrio, the cradle of the Puerto Rican community, Mexican bakeries, groceries, and butcher shops sprang up. Tiny *taquerias* sold beef tongue and barbecued-pork tacos to new customers, many of whom hailed from the central Mexican state of Puebla.

Goya now offers Mexicans a roster of seventy-five products, ranging from chili peppers and moles to cans of *menudo*, a tripe soup. Older items, such as pinto ("painted") beans, appeal to Mexicans, who prefer these New World legumes to Spanish chickpeas. For customers seeking convenience, Goya sells refried beans, ready to be folded into tacos or burritos.

Gradually, Goya tried to attract mainstream customers. Its first English-language television commercial in 1983 featured Hermione Gingold singing the wonders of Coca Goya, the cream of coconut used in piña coladas. In the 1990s, ads were run on *Northern Exposure, Roseanne, Murphy Brown*, and other programs with an upscale audience.

Promoting the nutritional value of its products in the media, Goya marketers believed, would help in capturing "crossover" customers. "Rice, beans, and olive oil are low in fats, high in fiber, protein, and essential acids and have assumed their rightful places on American dinner tables," a press release on Goya's sixtieth anniversary declared. A television spot that asked viewers, "Do you have a can of Goya beans in the house?" showed a Hispanic family extolling kidney beans to an American family. The goal of the advertising was to counter the image of beans as a "strange vegetarian food," Joseph Unanue noted.

Goya's desire to reach a wider audience sometimes clashed with its ambition to be the preeminent Latin food company. Executives dreamed of the American public embracing its cuisine: "Just the way Italian food is now, one day Spanish food will be American food," Joseph Unanue hoped. He felt the same lofty aspirations as his father: "Before he died, my father dreamed of the time when his company would not only become a well-known name in Latino homes, but also would be known to other segments of the American population."

But most of the company's energies were concentrated on perfecting its ethnic lines. Unlike Progresso, Goya still presented an alien face to many customers. Diluting the products' identity would mean losing its core Latin clientele. The separate Goya section in the supermarket represented one small aspect of the dilemma. Being "segregated from the normal foods . . . keeps people thinking we're just an ethnic food," Joseph Unanue reflected. "We try to keep our own section, and that way the Hispanic walks in and knows he's appreciated."

SOURCES

Overview

Very few full-length books have been written about the history of ethnic food, as distinct from cookbooks or other primers on international cuisines. The groundbreaker was James P. Shenton, ed., *American Cooking: The Melting Pot* (New York, 1971), which has exciting but limited text and lively pictures. I have learned a good deal from Donna R. Gabaccia, *We Are What We Eat: Ethnic Food and the Making of Americans* (Cambridge, 1998), a more analytical volume than my own. Although Raymond Sokolov, *Why We Eat What We Eat* (New York, 1991), concentrates on the Americas, his is a penetrating examination of the cultural roots of our food.

Elizabeth Rozin, *Ethnic Cuisine: The Flavor-Principle Cookbook* (Lexington, Mass., 1973), should be the starting point for any reader exploring ethnic food.

To understand ethnic food in the context of the history of American cooking, I have found Betty Fussell, *I Hear America Cooking* (New York, 1986), and Evan Jones, *American Food: The Gastronomic Story* (New York, 1981), to be very helpful chronicles. Waverly Root and Richard de Rochemont, *Eating in America* (Hopewell, N.J., 1985), a seminal work in food history, still offers valuable insights. One of the early histories of American foodways, Richard Hooker, *Food and Drink in America: A History* (New York, 1981), contains intriguing anecdotes and details. A scholarly investigation of the social foundations of American food can be found in two books by Harvey Levenstein, *Revolution at the Table: The Transformation of the American Diet* (New York, 1988) and *Paradox of Plenty: A Social History of Eating in Modern America* (New York, 1993).

Anyone writing food history needs to lean on some basic reference works. Indispensable is Alan Davidson, *The Oxford Companion to Food* (Oxford, 1999). For a single volume that stretches from the ancient to the modern world, see Reay Tannahill, *Food in History* (Briarcliff Manor, N.Y., 1973). To check any one of innumerable details and facts, consulting James Trager, *Food Chronology* (New York, 1995), is vital. A food reference standby is John F. Mariani, *The Dictionary of American Food and Drink* (New York, 1983).

Guidebooks, both those specializing in ethnic food and those focusing on the urban landscape, have stimulated my own interest and aroused my curiosity. Among the ones I hold dear are Milton Glaser and Jerome Snyder, *The Underground Gourmet* (New York, 1967); Zelda Stern, *The Complete Guide to Ethnic New York* (New York, 1980); Myra Alperson and Mark Clifford, *The Food Lover's Guide to the Real New York* (New York, 1987); Jim Leff, *The Eclectic Gourmet Guide to Greater New York City* (Birmingham, Ala., 1999); Robert Sietsema, *Good and Cheap Ethnic Eats in New York City* (New York, 1997); Ed Levine, *New York Eats* (New York, 1992); and Mark Leeds, *Ethnic New York* (Chicago, 1991). I wish to single out Kate Simon's lyrical evocation of New York City, *New York Places and Pleasures* (New York, 1971), which offers up many a sketch of the city's ethnicity.

I found several California guides very informative: R. B. Reid, *The San Francisco Underground Gourmet* (New York, 1977), a classic; Linda Buruma, *A Guide to Ethnic Food in Los Angeles* (New York, 1992); and Sharon Silva and Frank Viviano, *Exploring the Best Ethnic Restaurants of the Bay Area* (San Francisco, 1990), which stands out for its incisive observations on the interplay of food and culture.

Surveys of ethnic ingredients assisted me, including Lane Morgan, *The Ethnic Market Food Guide* (New York, 1997); Vilma Liacouras Chantiles, *The New York Ethnic Food Market Guide and Cookbook* (New York, 1984); and Irene Sax, *Cook's Marketplace, New York* (San Francisco, 1984). The bible in this area is Diana and Paul Von Welanetz, *The Welanetz Guide to Ethnic Ingredients* (New York, 1982).

To make this volume accessible to a general audience, I have not relied on the standard bibliographic format. Instead, I have included, by chapter, a general essay on sources that were helpful to me and may be of interest to readers who wish to explore the subject further. Also, specific citations have been limited to the sources of quotations, unless they were already identified in the text.

Chapter 1: That's Amore

For surveys of the Italian experience, read Humbert S. Nelli, *From Immigrants to Ethnics: The Italian Americans* (New York, 1983); Nelli, "Italians," in Stephen Thernstrom, ed., *Harvard Encyclopedia of American Ethnic Groups* (Cambridge, 1980); Andrew F. Rolle, *The American Italians: Their History and Culture* (Belmont, Calif., 1972); and Vincenza Scarpaci, *A Portrait of the Italians in America* (New York, 1982), which combines lively text and vivid photographs. Robert Forester, *Italian Emigration in Our Time* (New York, 1969), covers the American Italians in his survey of this immigrant diaspora. Eliot Lord, *The Italians in America* (New York, 1905), writes from a contemporary vantage point. Readers interested in a collection of primary source documents that contains intriguing selections should turn to Salvatore Mondello, *The Italian Immigrant in Urban*

America (New York, 1980). Alexander De Conde, *Half Bitter, Half Sweet: An Excursion into Italian-American History* (New York, 1971), conveys tantalizing information.

Two books, the first a memoir, the second a sociological study, offer incisive comments on Italian food traditions: Angelo Pellegrini, *The Unprejudiced Palate* (San Francisco, 1984), and Phyllis H. Williams, *South Italian Folkways in Europe and America* (New York, 1969).

Harvey Levenstein, a historian of American food, has written some of the most suggestive interpretations of Italian food and culture. Some of his best pieces are "The American Response to Italian Food, 1880–1930," *Food and Foodways*, vol. 1 (1985); "The Food Habits of Italian Immigrants to America: An Examination of the Persistence of a Food Culture and the Rise of 'Fast Food' in America," in Ray B. Browne, Marshall W. Fishwick, and Kevin O. Brown, eds., *Dominant Symbols in Popular Culture* (Bowling Green, Ohio, 1990); "The Food Habits of European Immigrants to America: Homogenization or Hegemonization," essay sent to author, undated.

A comprehensive portrait of the Italian food business is presented in Donna Gabaccia, "Ethnicity in the Business World: Italians in American Food Industries" (November 1997), copy of a lecture sent to author. Gabaccia's *You Are What You Eat* (1998) is chock full of leads to pursue about Italian food merchants.

The Italian journey in California, although not widely known, has received considerable scholarly attention. One of the early histories to set sights on immigrants in the West was Andrew F. Rolle. His volume, *The Immigrant Upraised* (Norman, Okla., 1968), lays an excellent foundation. An exhaustive investigation of Italian farming in the state is Hans Christian Palmer, "Italian Immigration and the Development of California Agriculture," Ph.D. dissertation, University of California, Berkeley, 1965. Vincenza Scarpaci, "Italians on the Land," unpublished manuscript sent to the author, reviews Italian contributions to agriculture in California and other regions.

Italians in the San Francisco Bay area have been the focus of a variety of observant writings: Raymond Dondero, *The Italian Settlement of San Francisco* (Saratoga, N.Y., 1950); Dino Cincel, *From Italy to San Francisco: The Immigrant Experience* (Palo Alto, 1982); Richard Dillon, *North Beach* (San Francisco, 1985); Rose Scherini, *The Italian American Community* (San Francisco, 1980); and Deanna Paoli Gumina, *The Italians of San Francisco* (New York, 1985). Felice Bonadio, *A. P. Giannini: Banker of America* (Berkeley, 1994), although primarily a biography of the San Francisco banker, is also a fine source on the immigrant community in the city and its businessmen. Sebastian Fichera, "Entrepreneurial Behavior in an Immigrant Colony: The Economic Experience of San Francisco's

Italian Americans 1850–1940," *Studi Emigrazione,* vol. 32, no. 118 (1995), examines the distinctiveness of ethnic business in the San Francisco enclave.

For the D'Arrigos, I have relied on historical material supplied by the company as well as the survey in Palmer (1965), which first alerted me to the business's importance. Two investigations of the D'Arrigos' marketing strategy are "D'Arrigo Brothers Company, Advertising of Branded Fresh Vegetables," in Neil Borden, *Advertising: Text and Cases* (Chicago, 1950), and "Branded Broccoli Brings Premium Prices for D'Arrigo Brothers," *Sales Management,* vol. 54, no. 7 (April 1, 1945). "D'Arrigo Bros. Co. of California Celebrates Its Diamond Anniversary," Anniversary Pamphlet, n.d., contains a useful history of the enterprise.

Di Giorgio, the agricultural titan, not widely enough known, is examined in Gabaccia (1997, 1998) and Palmer (1965). A wealth of information on his career is brought together in a University of California oral history, Robert Di Giorgio and Joseph A. Di Giorgio, *The Di Giorgios: From Fruit Merchants to Corporate Innovators* (Regional Oral History Office, The Bancroft Library, University of California, Berkeley, 1986). Two valuable articles are "The Fruit King," *Time,* vol. 47, no. 10 (March 11, 1946), and "Joseph Di Giorgio," *Fortune,* vol. 34, no. 2 (August 1946). Two volumes include useful material on the grower's Western empire: John Gregory Dunne, *Delano* (New York, 1967), and Dan Morgan, *Rising in the West* (New York, 1992).

The indispensable study on Italians in Louisiana and New Orleans is Jean Ann Scarpaci, "Italian Immigrants in Louisiana's Sugar Parishes: Recruitment, Labor Conditions, and Community Relations, 1880–1910," Ph.D. dissertation, Rutgers University, 1972. For the citrus heritage on which the Sicilians in New Orleans drew, see S. Tolkowski, *Hesperides: A History of the Culture and Use of Citrus Fruits* (London, 1938). The history and culture of New Orleans's Italian community are ably discussed by two Italian-American sociologists, A. V. Margavio and Jerome Salomone, "The Passage, Settlement, and Occupational Characteristics of Louisiana's Italian Immigrants," *Sociological Spectrum,* vol. 1 (1981). Russell Magnaghi, "Louisiana's Italian Immigrants Prior to 1870," *Louisiana History,* vol. 27, no. 1 (Winter 1986), uncovers the history of early Italian settlement. Richard Gambino, *Vendetta* (Garden City, N.Y., 1977), whose centerpiece is the notorious 1891 lynching of Italians in New Orleans, gathers compelling material on the ethnics and their lives in the Crescent City. A brief memoir on the families behind Standard Fruit is Joseph D'Antoni, "The Fascinating Vaccaro D'Antoni Story," n.d., an unpublished document sent to the author by Joseph Maselli of the American Italian Federation, New Orleans.

An acute essay on New Orleans's immigrant populations is Joseph Logsdon, "Immigration Through the Port of New Orleans," in M. Mark Stolarik, ed., *Forgotten Doors* (Philadelphia, 1988). Interviews with Logsdon and Anthony Margavio, two scholars of New Orleans's ethnic communities, were invaluable.

Giuseppe Uddo, the patriarch of Progresso, has been an invisible figure in the history of Italian immigration. My conversations with Frank Uddo, Giuseppe's son; Frank's son, Michael; and John Taormina, the son of a partner of the Uddos, were fascinating entrées into the history of the business. For important details about the Vaccaros and Standard Fruit, see Thomas L. Karnes, *Standard Fruit and Steamship Company in Latin America* (Baton Rouge, La., 1978). Emily Meade (Margaret Mead's daughter), *The Italians on the Land* (Hammonton, N.J., 1972), sketches Italian immigrant farmers in Hammonton, New Jersey, an area close to where Progresso located its plant.

Among the very few newspaper articles on the Uddo saga is "The Italians: An Immigrant's History Is Part of the Heritage of New Orleans," *Times-Picayune*, August 25, 1980. "The Uddo Family," *Italian-American Digest*, March 1977, is a brief family history. The Progresso division of the Pillsbury Company provided the author a chronology of the enterprise's history.

Quotation sources for Chapter 1:
Page
7   "rich earthy smell": Dillon 1985, p. 72.
11   "perfect method of distribution": Di Giorgio and Di Giorgio 1986, p. 7.
12   "earliness of maturity": Ibid., p. 7.
12   "twenty-horse mule teams": Ibid., p. 75.
13   "shelf life": Ibid., p. 162.
14   "salvage your own": Ibid., p. 132.
15   "blazing fire": Tolkowski 1938, p. 116.
15   "recreated their world": Interview Joseph Logsdon.
15–16 "Italian enterprise and capital": Scarpaci 1972, pp. 58–59.
16   "monopolize the fruit, oyster . . . ": Gambino 1977, p. 18.
17   "the only wagon there": "The Fascinating Vaccaro," n.d., n.p.
17   "coconuts and bananas in Honduras": Ibid.
18   "out of the mud": Karnes 1978, p. 102.
19   "the waste fields": Scarpaci 1972, p. 34.
19   "they have laid by a little money": Ibid., p. 211.
20   "riot of smells": Gambino 1977, p. 50.
21   "The roads were terrible": *New Orleans Times-Picayune*, November 29, 1981.
24   "popularized the sweet pepper": Meade 1972, p. 18.

Chapter 2: From the Fertile Crescent

The summa of Middle Eastern food books is Claudia Roden, *A New Book of Middle East Food* (New York, 1985), a volume that masterfully blends recipes, food history, and cultural perspective. Her *Mediterranean Cooking* (London, 1987) also contains sharp insights into the region's food. Other valuable books on this cuisine include Paula Wolfert, *Mediterranean Cooking* (New York, 1977); Mary Laird Hamady, *Lebanese Mountain Cookery* (Boston, 1987); Harry G. Nickles, *Middle Eastern Cooking* (New York, 1969); Arto der Haroutunian, *Middle Eastern Cooking* (London, 1984); and Sonia Uvezian, *The Cuisine of Armenia* (New York, 1974).

Some authors concentrate on the historical roots of Arabic food. Andrew M. Watson, *Agricultural Innovation in the Early Islamic World* (Cambridge, 1983), is a groundbreaking account of the dispersal of Arabic foodstuffs throughout the Arabs' dominions. Clifford A. Wright, *A Mediterranean Feast* (New York, 1999), contains both recipes and genealogies of Middle Eastern cooking. For classic Arabic recipes from previously untranslated cookbooks and penetrating commentary, see Maxine Rodinson, A. J. Arberry, and Charles Perry, *Medieval Arab Cookery* (Devon, England, 2001).

There is a growing literature on the history of Arab immigration to the United States. Good starting points are Alixa Naff, *Becoming American: The Early Arab Immigrant Experience* (Carbondale, Ill., 1985), and her "Arabs," in Stephen Thernstrom, ed., *Harvard Encyclopedia of American Ethnic Groups* (Cambridge, 1980). Valuable nuggets on ethnic history are unearthed in Gregory Orfalea, *Before the Flames: A Quest for the History of Arab Americans* (Austin, Tex., 1988). Philip M. Kayal and Joseph M. Kayal, *The Syrian-Lebanese in America* (Boston, 1975), is chock full of sociological and historical insights. Walter Zenner, "Arabic-Speaking Immigrants in North America," *Ethnic and Racial Studies*, vol. 5, no. 4 (1982), is an informative article on the experience of Middle Eastern settlers. A useful collection of studies on Arabic immigrants is assembled in Eric Hooglund, ed., *Crossing the Waters: Arabic-Speaking Immigrants to the United States Before 1940* (Washington, D.C., 1987). S. Y. Abraham and Abraham N. Abraham, *Arabs in the New World: Studies in Arab-American Communities* (Detroit, 1983), and Barbara C. Aswad, *Arabic-Speaking Communities in American Cities* (New York, 1980), pull together intriguing portraits of the Middle Eastern immigrant story.

Notable chronicles of Armenians are Robert Mirak, *Torn Between Two Lands: Armenians in America, 1890 to World War I* (Cambridge, Mass., 1983), and Armenian Historical Society, *Armenians in Massachusetts* (Boston, 1937).

An early depiction of the Syrian community in New York City is Lucius Hopkins Miller, *Our Syrian Population* (San Francisco, 1969). A luscious portrait of

Washington Street is in Will Irwin, *Highlights of Manhattan* (New York, 1926). The wide-ranging volume by Konrad Bercovici, *Around the World in New York* (New York, 1924), has an absorbing chapter on the Syrians. The most recent attempt to reconstruct the history of New York City's Arabic immigrants is Kathleen Benson and Philip M. Kayal, eds., *A Community of Many Worlds: Arab Americans in New York City* (Syracuse, N.Y., 2002); particularly helpful in this volume is Mary Ann Haick DiNapoli, "The Syrian-Lebanese Community of South Ferry from Its Origin to 1977." A nice portrait of Washington Street baker Nuah Abaid is "A Magic Carpet in a Sweets-Shop," *New York World-Telegram*, March 6, 1937.

My interviews with Charles Sahadi, the late Joe Shuad, Robert Colombosian, Omar Elshafey, and George Rababy were critical sources.

One of the few pieces to chronicle the Colombosians is Joan Nathan, "A 6,000 Year Culture," *Boston Globe*, October 15, 1978. Materials on Colombo provided by the Andover, Massachusetts, Historical Society were also helpful.

Quotation sources for Chapter 2:
Page
27   "Tins of olive oil": Irwin 1926, p. 32.
27   "red fezzes": Kayal and Kayal 1975, p. 99.
28   "It was a gold rush": Naff 1985, p. 91.
28   "dumping ground for new arrivals": Miller 1969, p. 18.
28   "swarthy men": Bercovici 1924, p. 27.
30   "pins by the hundred": Naff 1985, p. 137.
31   "stinks and smells": Mirak 1983, p. 94.
34   "Haddads from Jersey City": "Casbah in Brooklyn," Merle Goldberg, *New York*, July 14, 1969.

Chapter 3: "Cheezborga, Cheezborga, Cheezborga, No Coke, Pepsi"

The dean of historians of Greek immigration was the late Theodore Saloutous, author of the comprehensive *Greeks in the United States* (Cambridge, 1964). Theodore Saloutous, "Greeks," in Stephan Thernstrom, ed., *Harvard Encyclopedia of American Ethnic Groups* (Cambridge, 1980), is a concise introduction to the subject. Charles Moskos, *Greek Americans, Struggle and Success* (New Brunswick, N.J., 1989), combines both history and sociological perspective in his study of this ethnic group. An older history, though still pertinent, is Thomas Burgess, *Greeks in America* (New York, 1970). Two volumes by contemporary observers of the early Greek wave are Edward A. Steiner, *On the Trail of the Immigrant* (New York, 1960), and Henry Fairchild, *Greek Immigration to the United States* (New Haven, Conn., 1911).

Chicago's Greek community is investigated in Andrew Kopan, "Greek Survival in Chicago," in Melvin Holli and Peter d'A. Jones, eds., *Ethnic Chicago* (Grand Rapids, Mich., 1995). Kopan's "Yasso! A Toast to Good Health," *Illinois Food Service News* (April–May 1983), is a useful survey of the Greek food business in Chicago. Alexander Rassogianis, *The Growth of Greek Business in Chicago 1900–1930*, M.A. thesis, University of Wisconsin, Milwaukee, 1982, is full of telling details about Greek entrepreneurial ventures in this immigrant bastion. A comprehensive guidebook to Chicago with good material on Greeks is Jory Graham, *Chicago: An Extraordinary Guide* (Chicago, 1967).

For an interesting portrait of Greeks in New York City, see Konrad Bercovici, *Around the World in New York* (New York, 1924).

No one has written a history of the prominent role that Greeks played in the candy business. There is indispensable material in the cited volumes by Saloutous and Moskos and in the essay by Kopan. Peter Dickson, "The Greek Pilgrims: Tsakonas and Tsintzinians," in Dan Georgakas and Charles C. Moskos, eds., *New Directions in Greek American Studies* (New York, 1991), is an intriguing essay on Christos Tsakonas, the Greek candy entrepreneur. A fascinating sidebar to Chicago candy history is the tale of the Dove bar told in "Chicago's Dove Bars: Taking Wing," *Washington Post*, September 18, 1985. My interview with Jimmy Mezilson was helpful on the Greek candy business in Chicago.

An abundance of writing has been done on the Greek coffee shops and diners, primarily in newspapers and magazines. Among the more absorbing articles are "Where the Blue Paper Cups Are," *New York Times*, January 27, 1995; "Greek Diners, Where Anything Is Possible," *New York Times*, February 27, 1991; "Culinary Exploits of Homer's Sons," *New York Times*, October 25, 2000; "A Day in the Life of a Greek Diner," *New York Daily News*, March 1, 1999; "Counter Culture: Greek Diners in New York," *Odyssey*, April/May 1994; and "The Old-Country Network," *Wall Street Journal*, May 20, 1985. *The Estiator*, a monthly magazine on the Greek food industry, is a useful guide. *Roadside* is a newspaper that follows the diner business.

Invaluable were interviews with people who had firsthand experience of the Greek diner/restaurant business. My discussions with Marios Christodoulides, George Vallianos, Richard Gutman, and Harold Kullman helped me grasp the industry. An interview with Wayne Meadowcroft, vice president of sales and marketing for the Sherri company, shed light on the Greek coffee cup. Diner history is chronicled in Richard J. S. Gutman, *American Diner Then and Now* (New York, 1993); Peter Genovese, *Jersey Diners* (New Brunswick, N.J., 1996); and Joseph T. Manzo, "From Pushcart to Modular Restaurant: The Diner on the Landscape," in Barbara G. Shortridge and James R. Shortridge, eds., *The Taste of American Place: A Reader on Regional and Ethnic Foods* (Lanham, Md., 1988).

One on Every Corner: Manhattan's Greek-Owned Coffee Shops, a film by Doreen Moses and Andrea Hull (Washington, D.C., 1984), captures the New York City coffee shop more vividly than any written account.

An intriguing analysis of the Greek role in the pizza business is Lawrence A. Lovell-Troy, "Ethnic Occupational Structures: Greeks in the Pizza Business," *Ethnicity*, vol. 8, no. 1 (1981). Another valuable essay by this scholar is Lawrence A. Lovell-Troy, "Clan Structure and Economic Activity: The Case of Greeks in Small Business Enterprise," in Scott Cummings, *Self-Help in Urban America: Patterns of Minority Business Enterprise* (Port Washington, N.Y., 1980).

Quotation sources for Chapter 3:
Page
47   "dried vegetables": Steiner 1960, p. 290.
47   "dark and mustached sons": Holli and Jones 1995, p. 522.
49   "Graeco-Roman wars": Holli and Jones 1995, p. 277.
49   "Italian stores": Bercovici 1924, p. 65.
50–51 "every busy corner": Saloutous 1964, p. 262.
51   "burning our hands": *Washington Post*, September 18, 1985.
52   "Americanize ourselves": Saloutous 1964, p. 263.
53   "stamberry pie": Graham 1967, p. 353.
53   "Pure American": Saloutous 1964, p. 269.
56   "diners were sold by the running foot": Genovese 1996, p. 23.
58   "sending a telegram": *New York Times*, February 27, 1991.
59–60 Zanikos quotations from the film *One on Every Corner*.
60   "You go to the coffee man": Ibid.
60   "cantaloupe and Jell-O": *New York Times*, October 25, 2000.
61   "Everyone wants that cup": *New York Times*, January 27, 1995.
62   "I gave my reputation to him": Cummings 1980, p. 81.
63   "long hours, lots of work": *New York Daily News*, March 21, 1999.
63   "ad in a Korean newspaper": *Wall Street Journal*, May 20, 1985.

Chapter 4: The "Heartburn of Nostalgia"

Two substantial overviews of Jewish cooking and culture are Joan Nathan, *Jewish Cooking in America* (New York, 1988), and Claudia Roden, *The Book of Jewish Food* (New York, 1996). Two valuable sources on the eastern European background to Jewish food are John Cooper, *Eat and Be Satisfied: A Social History of Jewish Food* (Northvale, N.J., 1993), and Mary Zborowski and Elizabeth Herzog, *Life Is with People: The Culture of the Shtetl* (New York, 1952). Jenna Weissman Joselit, *The Wonders of America* (New York, 1994), an excellent examination of Jewish culture, offers superb discussions of Jewish foodways. A wonderful combination of humor, reminiscence, and history, Israel Shenker, *Noshing Is Sacred* (Indianapolis, Ind., 1979), introduced me to the Gabay story and provided me with the title for this chapter. Ruth Gay, *Unfinished People: Eastern European Jews Encounter America* (New York, 1996), combines memoir with perceptive views on the Jewish culinary tradition. For a good primer on Jewish food, see Patti Shosteck, *A Lexicon of Jewish Cooking* (Chicago, 1981).

The Lower East Side's Jewish culture and folkways have been written about extensively. Among the many informative volumes are Ronald Sanders, *Lower East Side* (New York, 1979); Hasia Diner, Jeffrey Shandler, Beth S. Wenger, eds., *Remembering the Lower East Side* (Bloomington, Ind., 2000); and Allan Schoener, *Portal to America: The Lower East Side 1870–1925* (New York, 1967). Moses Rischin, *The Promised City: New York's Jews* (New York, 1962), is an excellent history of the New York City Jewish community that contains valuable information on the Lower East Side. Fred Ferretti beautifully capsulizes the food scene in "New York's Lower East Side," *Gourmet* (October 1986). For a lively article on seltzer, see "Seltzer Keeps Bubbling," *New York Times*, August 21, 1974.

Memoirs by Jewish immigrants shed important light on the Lower East Side experience. I have learned from Harry Golden, *The Greatest Jewish City in the World* (New York, 1972), and M. E. Ravage, *An American in the Making: The Life Story of an Immigrant* (New York, 1971). The oral history of New York City produced by Jeff Kisseloff, *You Must Remember This* (New York, 1989), includes reminiscences of the Lower East Side on which I have drawn.

Other books that deal only in part with the Lower East Side are Kate Simon's guidebook (1971) referred to in the introduction; Richard F. Shepard and Vicki Gold Levi, *Live and Be Well* (New York, 1982), which gathers Shepard's (the late *New York Times* reporter who covered New York's Jewish community) unparalleled knowledge of the subject; and the Time-Life volume *American Cooking: The Melting Pot* (in the introduction, New York, 1971), especially the essay by James P. Shenton. For a useful guide to Jewish New York, including sites on the Lower East Side, see Bernard Postal and Leonard Koppman, *Jewish Landmarks in New York* (New York, 1964).

The Lower East Side's foodways are pictured in Milton Glaser's and Jerome Snyder's *Underground Gourmet* (1967, listed in the introduction). A history of Ratner's, the venerable dairy restaurant, would be an engrossing book; I gleaned vital details about its history from the column by Nat Presser, "Cordially Yours," in *East Side News*, November 23, 1962. Judith Gethers and Elizabeth Lefft, *Ratner's Meatless Cookbook* (New York, 1975), collects many of the eatery's classic recipes. A nostalgic piece on the closing of a garment-center restaurant is "Culinary Era Is Ended by DuBrow's," *New York Times*, August 3, 1985.

Sue Kreitzman, *Deli* (New York, 1985), is a fount of delicatessen lore. Historical notes on the origins of the deli are recounted in L. H. Robins, "Rest for the Delicatessen," *New York Times*, August 15, 1937. A piece by Joseph Berger, "As Delis Dwindle, Traditions Lose Bite," *New York Times*, May 15, 1996, reports on the transformation of the New York City delicatessen. Alfred Kazin, *A Walker in the City* (New York, 1951), a rhapsodic memoir of growing up in Brownsville (a neighborhood in Brooklyn), has wonderful descriptions of the delicatessen. Other than its fictional chronicler, Damon Runyon, Lindy's has not found the historian it deserves. An amusing sketch of Lindy's can be found in the late entertainment reporter Robert Sylvester's *Notes of a Guilty Bystander* (Englewood Cliffs, N.J., 1970). A fascinating interview with Arnold Reuben is "Reuben and His Restaurant," part of the *American Life Histories: Manuscripts from the Federal Writers' Project, 1936–1940* at the Library of Congress (Washington, D.C., 1938).

Of the numerous accounts of Nathan's, most helpful were Murray Handwerker, *Nathan's Famous Hot Dog Cookbook* (New York, 1983), and Edo McCullough, *Good Old Coney Island* (New York, 2000), which deals with both Nathan's and Feltman's in the context of the larger saga of Coney Island. An insightful piece by Jenna Weissman Joselit, "Home Plate and Hot Dogs Are Like Ball and Glove When Summer Hits," *Jewish Forward*, July 12, 2002, points out the bonds between Yiddish popular culture and the world of Coney Island.

Among the numerous website pieces with useful information on Nathan's and hot-dog history are Jeffrey Stanton, "Coney Island—Food and Dining," online at http://naid.sppsr.ucla.edu/coneyisland/articles/food.htm; National Hot Dog and Sausage Council, "History of the Hot Dog," online at www.hot-dog.org/hd_history.htm; and Linda Stradley, "History and Legends of Hot Dogs," online at http://whatscookingamerica.net/History/HotDog/HDHistory.htm. An insightful exploration of hot-dog history is Bruce Kraig, "The American Hot Dog: Standardized Taste and Regional Variations," in Tom Jaine, ed., *Oxford Symposium 1987: Taste* (London, 1988).

Two revealing portraits of Nathan Handwerker are "Famous Nathan," *New York Times*, August 3, 1966, and "A Man, a Plan, a Hot Dog: Birth of a Nathan's," *New York Times*, January 25, 1998.

Breakstone's story has not received the attention it deserves. Interviews with Dr. Stanley Leavy and the late Sanford Claster helped me unravel the family and business history. Dr. Leavy kindly lent me a family history, Jeffrey A. Marx and Walter B. Miller, *A History of the Breakstone/Breghstein Family* (February 1993). Rabbi Marx provided valuable details about the Breakstones. He also gave me his "Breakstone Brothers Dairy Chronology," which covers the business's development with precision (personal communication with author, January 2003).

The Sara Lee Corporation, whose significance Joan Nathan's book (1988) alerted me to, sent me historical materials about Charles Lubin and Sara Lee, including the revealing "Our Story" (n.d.). I learned about the Gabay story from Israel Shenker's *Noshing Is Sacred* (1979) and pursued it with interviews with Elliott Gabay, grandson of founder Elias.

Uncovering the Vita saga, which has been largely invisible, required much investigation. I was able to track down Aaron Gilman, the son-in-law of cofounder Victor Heller, who filled me in on critical information about the business. Little has been written about Vita. Two informative articles are the obituary of Victor Heller, "Victor A. Heller, Headed Vita Food," *New York Times*, January 1, 1968, and Richard B. Gehman, "Fish 'n' Smoke," *Nation's Business*, vol. 40, no. 6 (June 1952). An overview of Vita's current business is presented in J. M. Dutton Associates, "Research Report," May 6, 2002.

Quotation sources for Chapter 4:
Page
   65   "jabbered," "jostled": Schoener 1967, p. 56.
   66   "comely young woman": Cooper 1993, p. 149.
   66   "highly flavored relishes": Zborowski and Herzog 1952, p. 371.
   67   "After he buys 'em": Kisseloff 1989, p. 43.
   67   "worse than dying," Shenker 1979, p. 27.
   67   "Big fish and little fish": Schoener 1967, p. 56.
 67–68 "herring every day": Kisseloff 1989, p. 42.
   68   "peculiar love for highly seasoned foods": Joselit 1994, p. 203.
   69   "On Sunday rich people": Glaser and Snyder 1967, p. 206.
   72   "It was a meeting place": *New York Times*, August 3, 1985.
   73   "weaned on this stuff": Nathan 1988, p. 377.
   74   "strong German accent": *New York Times*, August 15, 1937.
   74   "Rumanian deli store": Ravage 1971, p. 88.
   75   "panting for the hot dogs": Kazin 1951, p. 34.
   77   "open your place": Handwerker 1983, p. xxi.
   77   "Hey, Nathan, you're getting famous": Ibid., p. xxii.
   77   "come with stethoscopes": Ibid.
   78   "At Coney Island you can buy": *Jewish Forward*, July 12, 2002.

78   "shrieked like fire engine sirens": McCullough 2000, p. 244.
79   "No man can hope to get elected": *New York Times*, August 3, 1966.
79   "Broadway nervous tempo manner": "Reuben and His Restaurant," p. 3.
79   "little shtoonky delicatessen store": Ibid.
79–80 "I only ate hamburgers": Nathan 1988, p. 184.
80   "maze of nonsense": Sylvester 1970, p. 222.
81   "fresh, white cheeses": Gay 1996, p. 171.
82   "wonderful wooden boxes of cream cheese": Marx and Miller 1993, p. AII:24.
83   "making it with cottage cheese": Nathan 1988, p. 334.
83   "sounds wholesome and American": Sara Lee Corp., "Our Story," p. 1.
84   "molds and pipes and transmission belts": Shenker 1979, p. 93.
88   "quality line of kosher products": J. M. Dutton 2002, p. 3.

Chapter 5: From Chow Mein to Singapore Noodle

Among the host of histories of the Chinese immigrant experience, some place the story in the framework of the larger Asian ethnic saga. Some of the most valuable are Sucheng Chan, *Asian Americans: An Interpretive History* (Boston, 1991); B. L. Sung, *The Story of the Chinese in America* (New York, 1967); Jack Chen, *The Chinese of America* (San Francisco, 1989); and Stan Steiner, *Fusang* (New York, 1979). Sucheng Chan, *This Bittersweet Soil* (Berkeley, 1986), is not only a brilliant account of the role of Chinese in Western agriculture but also a gold mine of rich detail about Chinese immigrants.

Lynn Pan's *Sons of the Yellow Emperor* (New York, 1990) is a nicely written history of the Chinese disapora. It also contains useful nuggets about Chinese settlement in the United States. In *The Encyclopedia of the Chinese Overseas* (Cambridge, 1989), Pan presents a panoramic view of Chinese ethnicity that offers insights into patterns of immigration in America.

For a rich primer on the history of the Chinese in California, see Thomas W. Chinn, ed., *A History of the Chinese in California* (San Francisco, 1969). Writings on San Francisco's Chinatown abound. Mary Roberts Coolidge, *Chinese Immigration* (New York, 1969), an early study, is full of deftly written descriptions. For vivid portraits of life in this enclave, see Charles Caldwell Dobie, *San Francisco's Chinatown* (New York, 1936), and Mary E. Bamford, *Ti: A Story of San Francisco's Chinatown* (Chicago, 1899). A basic introduction is Helen Virginia Cather, *The History of San Francisco's Chinatown* (San Francisco, 1974). Laverne Mau Dicker, *The Chinese in San Francisco: A Pictorial History* (New York, 1979), is full of intriguing photographs and historical material. Brian J. Godfrey, *Neighborhoods in Transition* (Berkeley and Los Angeles, 1988), investigates Chinatown as part of a larger study on San Francisco enclaves. For a predominantly sociological take on this Chinese community, see Chalisa M. Loo, *Chinatown Most Time Hard Time* (New York, 1991). Victor G. and Brett de Barry Nee gather informal oral histories in *Longtime Californ': A Documentary Study of an American Chinatown* (New York, 1973). A relatively recent study of San Francisco's Chinatown that emphasizes its cultural traditions is Yong Chen, *Chinese San Francisco* (Palo Alto, 2000).

Two articles that depict early Chinatown as well as immigrant foodways are James O'Meara, "Chinese in Early Days," *Overland Monthly*, vol. 8 (1884), and Idwal Jones, "Cathay on the Coast," *American Mercury*, vol. 8, no. 32 (August 1926).

Only a few scholars have dug deeply into the food businesses that supplied the immigrant community. Noteworthy studies are Robert F. Spier, "Food Habits of Nineteenth-Century California Chinese," *California Historical Society Quarterly*, vol. 37, no. 1 (March 1958); L. Eve Armentrout Ma, "The Big Business Ventures of Chinese in North America," in Ginny Lim, ed., *The Chinese American Experience* (San Francisco, 1980); and Ma, "Big and Medium Businesses of Chinese Immigrants to the United States, 1850–1890," *Bulletin Chinese Historical Society of America*, vol. 13, no. 7 (September 1978).

Two essays probe the basic provisions that Chinese stores supplied their immigrant clientele. William S. Evans, Jr., "Food and Fantasy: Material Culture of the Chinese in California and the West," and Paul E. Langenwalter II, "The Archaeology of Nineteenth-Century Chinese Subsistence at the Lower China Store, Madera County, California," appear in Robert Schuyler, ed., *Archaeological Perspectives on Ethnicity in America* (Farmingdale, N.Y., 1980).

An expanding exploration of the Chinese experience in the Western mines, railroads, and other industries is under way. Arif Dirlik, *Chinese on the American Frontier* (Lanham, Md., 2001); Liping Zhu, *A Chinaman's Chance* (Niwot, Colo., 1997); and Cathy Luchetti, *Home on the Range* (New York, 1983), are important contributions. The sections on the Chinese in Joseph Conlin, *Bacon, Beans, and Galantines* (Reno, Nev., 1986), present stunning vignettes.

For perspectives on the interplay between Chinese food and culture, incisive interpretations are K. C. Chang, ed., *Food in Chinese Culture* (New Haven, Conn., 1977), and E. N. Anderson, *The Food of China* (New Haven, Conn., 1988). There are keen comments on the history of Chinese food in the United States in Richard J. Hooker (1981, cited in the introduction).

A fascinating inquiry into chop suey is the piece by Rengiu Yu, "Chop Suey: From Chinese Food to Chinese American Food," in *Chinese America: History and Perspectives*, vol. 1 (San Francisco, 1987).

On Chinatown and Chinese business, sociologist Ivan Light has been a pioneer. His "From Vice District to Tourist Attraction: The Moral Career of American Chinatowns, 1880–1940," *Pacific Historical Review*, vol. 43 (1974), is invaluable. Ivan Light, *Ethnic Enterprise in America* (Berkeley, 1972), examines Chinese self-employment as an example of a larger trend. Bryan Johnson, "Chinese Tonight," *American Heritage* (December 1987), is studded with revealing examples of the struggle Chinese restaurants waged for acceptance. Peter Kwong, *The New Chinatown* (New York, 1987), spotlights changing social conditions in the New York City enclave.

Two volumes, a biography and an autobiography, are the best jumping-off points for understanding the career of Jeno Paulucci: L. E. Leipold, *Jeno F. Paulucci: Merchant Philanthropist* (Minneapolis, Minn., 1968), and Jeno Paulucci (with Les Rich), *How It Was to Make $100,000,000 in a Hurry: The Tale of Jeno and the Bean Sprout* (New York, 1969). Some of the most rewarding pieces on the promoter are "Jeno Paulucci: When Chop Suey and Pizza Aren't Enough," *Business Week*, February 29, 1988; Ellen Wojahn, "Little Big Man," *Manhattan Inc.* (June 1986); Christopher Evans, "The Paulucci Empire: From Father to Son," *The Minneapolis Star*, June 2, 1979; and Mike Pehanich, "Make Way for Jeno," *Prepared Foods* (February 1984). Caroline Wyman, *I'm a Spam Fan* (Stamford, Conn., 1993), a popular account of brand-name products, has a brief summary of Paulucci's achievements.

My ambles through Boston's Chinatown have helped me fathom this fascinating quarter. To delve into South Cove's history, browse through the Chinatown Heritage Trail at http://yerkes.mit.edu/Chinatown/time.html. Steve Johnson, "Chow Fun," *Boston Magazine* (September 2000), guides readers on an excursion through the neighborhood. A March 9, 1997, article in the *Boston Globe* focuses on the rejuvenation of Chinatown: "Chinatown Enjoys a Renaissance."

Fred Ferretti, "The Nonya Kitchen of Singapore," *Gourmet* (September 1986), is an excellent introduction to the melding of Chinese and Malay cooking. L. N. Anderson and Marja L. Anderson, "Penang Hokkien Ethno-hoptology," *Ethnos*, vol. 37 (1972), is an anthropological investigation of Chinese foodways in Malaysia. For an analysis of Chinese immigration to Singapore, see Maurice Freedman, "Immigrants and Associations: Chinese in Nineteenth-Century Singapore," in Lloyd Fallers, *Immigrants and Associations* (Paris, 1967).

The two volumes by Pan are good sources on the Chinese migration in Southeast Asia. Edgar Wickberg, "The Chinese as Overseas Migrants," in Judith M. Brown, ed., *Migration: The Asian Experience* (New York, 1994), is a concise, helpful analysis of the overseas Chinese.

A recent volume, David Y. H. Wu and Tan Chee-beng, *Changing Chinese Foodways in Asia* (Hong Kong, 2001), focuses on Southeast Asian cooking in a few of its contributions. Cookbooks on the region with perceptive insights include Rafi Fernandez, *Malaysian Cookery* (Middlesex, England, 1985); Copeland Marks, *The Indonesian Kitchen* (New York, 1981); and Djoko Wibisono, *The Food of Singapore* (Singapore, 1995).

Quotation sources for Chapter 5:
Page
  90–91 "huge basket hats": Chinn 1969, p. 30.
    92   "they are quiet, peaceable": Jack Chen 1989, p. 68.
    92   "swarmed with Celestials": Dicker 1979, p. 9.
    93   "they breathe easier": Yong Chen 2000, p. 60.
    94   "stocked with hams, tea": Chinn 1969, p. 10.
    94   "toys, peanuts, dry lichees,": Pan 1990, p. 100.
    95   "the Chinese are filthy": Steiner 1979, pp. 196–197.
    94   "fat tubs of cold clammy rice": Dobie 1936, p. 225.
    94   "beans in sprouting condition": Ibid., p. 261.
  94–95 "yellow squares of bean curd": Bamford 1899, p. 20.
    95   "why you're not Charlie": Conlin 1986, p. 189.
    96   "smoky lairs": Jones 1926, p. 455.
    96   "best eating houses in San Francisco": Conlin 1986, p. 193.
    96   "pale cakes with a waxen look": Bryan Johnson 1987, p. 100.
    97   "gleams at night": Ibid., p. 10.
    98   "mess of veal": Hooker 1981, p. 287.
    98   "rats, cats, and puppies": Light 1974, p. 378.
    99   "laboring classes and outlaws": Jones 1926, p. 10.
    99   "stale odors, sprawling drunks": Ibid., p. 386.
    99   "seeing Chinatown at night": Light 1974, p. 389.
    99   "chief jewel": Ibid., p. 391.
   100   "juke and soup joints": Nee 1973, p. 115.
   100   "bathed in red iron dust": Paulucci 1969, p. 12.
   100   "flat full of cockroaches": Ibid., p. 12.
   101   "ready to yell my lungs out": Ibid., p. 18.
   101   "How much garlic": Wyman 1993, p. 65.
   102   "with so many young men": Ibid., p. 30.
   103   "pretty bland sort of thing": Leipold 1968, p. 119.
   103   "with those peppers": Paulucci 1969, p. 129.
   103   "rich imperial sound": Ibid., p. 38.

104 "This looks so delicious": Ibid., p. 37.
105 "Only in America": Leipold 1968, p. 6.
109 "circled by mountains": Pan 1989, p. 30.
109 "sea was paddy": Ibid., p. 30.
109 "refugees from official displeasure": Freedman 1967, p. 18.

Chapter 6: Currying Favor

An understanding of Indian life and culture can be gleaned from travel guides and more formal chronicles. John Keay, *Into India* (London, 1985); Louise Nicholson, *India* (Boston, 1975); and Lonely Planet's *India Travel Survival Kit* (Victoria, Australia, 1984) are fine examples of such writing. On Pakistan, Stephen Alter, *Amritsar to Lahore* (Philadelphia, 2001); Arnold J. Toynbee, *Between Oxus and Jumma* (New York, 1961); and Richard Reeves, *Passage to Peshawar* (New York, 1984), offer suggestive glimpses.

There is a wealth of cookbooks on Indian food. Particularly useful are the discussions in Jennifer Brennan, *Cuisines of Asia* (New York, 1994); and Madhur Jaffrey, *An Invitation to Indian Cooking* (New York, 1975) and *A Taste of India* (New York, 1988). Santha Rama Rau, *The Cooking of India* (New York, 1975), is part of the fine Time-Life series on international cuisines. Julie Sahni, *Classic Indian Cookery* (New York, 1980), concentrates on Northern cuisine. K. T. Achaya, *Indian Food: A Historical Companion* (Delhi, 1974), analyzes Indian food in historical context. For intensive cultural anatomies of the subcontinent's food, see Arjun Appadurai, "How to Make a National Cuisine: Cookbooks in Contemporary India," in *Comparative Studies in Society and History,* vol. 30 (1988), and Hashi Raychaudhuri and Tapan Raychaudhuri, "Not by Curry Alone," in Alan Davidson, ed., *Oxford Symposium 1981* (London, 1981). A suggestive essay on the kebab is Claudia Roden, "The Spread of Kebabs and Coffee: Two Islamic Movements," in Alan Davidson, ed., *Oxford Symposium 1983* (London, 1983).

Moghul food is brilliantly reviewed in Joyce Westrip, *Moghul Cooking* (London, 1997). Babur's memoirs, which are contained in Wheeler M. Thackston, ed., *The Baburnama* (New York, 1966), recount the emperor's encounter with India. Abdul Shalim Sharar, *Lucknow: The Last Phase of an Oriental Culture* (Bombay, 1989), illuminates the Moghul culture of this Indian city. "Kabobs and Breads of Lucknow," *New York Times*, February 25, 1990, is a fascinating piece on the food lore of this Moghul city.

On the role of Bangladeshis in the British food business, see Caroline Adams, ed., *Across Seven Seas and Thirteen Rivers* (London, 1987). The *Time Out Eating and Drinking Guide 2002* (London, 2001) discusses the Bangladeshi contribution in its overview of Indian food. Several pieces have sketched the "Indian" restaurants run by Bangladeshis in New York City, one by Fred Ferretti, *New York Times*, March 4, 1981, and another by Barbara Crossette, *New York Times*, April 7, 2000. An article in the online publication *NYC24*, issue 1, "Business First for Bangladesh," by Irene Muchemi and Michael Yeh, available at http://www.nyc24.com/2000/issue01/story06/page3.html, deals with Bangladeshi restaurateurs.

An encyclopedic introduction to Indian vegetarian food is Julie Sahni, *Classic Indian Vegetarian and Grain Cooking* (New York, 1985).

I have not unearthed a cookbook on Pakistan alone. Many of the cookbooks on North Indian food previously listed provide insight into the dishes the two countries share. A recent article by Madhur Jaffrey, "A Passage to Pakistan," *Saveur* (September–October 2002), highlights Punjabi and frontier cooking.

India Abroad, the weekly newspaper aimed at the Indian immigrant community in America, covers a wide range of topics, including food, important to ethnics. Two informative papers that cover the Pakistani community are the *New York Awam* and the *Weekly Magazine News Pakistan*, published in Alexandria, Virginia.

Interviews and conversations with Mohammed Afzal and his brother, Tariq, along with countless visits to their Ravi Kabob House restaurant, were essential to the kebab section.

Quotation sources for Chapter 6:
Page
116   "Hindustan is a place": Thackston 1966, p. 350.
117   "100 elephants": Rau 1975, p. 158.
118   "Rice boiled so artificially": Jaffrey 1988, p. 24.
119   "shining pearls": Sharar 1989, p. 162.
119   "auspicious arrival": Westrip 1997, p. 18.
121   "yolks of a hundred eggs": Jaffrey 1988, p. 52.
121–122 "people kept knocking": *New York Times*, March 4, 1981.
122   "very quickly we make good money": Ibid.
122   "Bangladesh is a small country": *NYC24*, issue 1.
122–123 "95% of New York's Indian restaurants": *New York Times*, April 7, 2000.
123   "pots of various stocks": *Time Out Guide*, p. 75.
123   "opportunities in America": *New York Times*, April 7, 2000.
132   "slaughter of animals": Alter 2001, p. 106.

Chapter 7: Papaya and Plantain

Chili, both the spice and the American dish, has inspired a mountain of writing. Jean Andrews, *Peppers* (Austin, Tex., 1995), is an encyclopedic survey of the chili in all its dimensions. Her piece "The Peripatetic Chili Pepper: Diffusion of the Domesticated Capsicums Since Columbus," in Nelson Foster and Linda Cordell, eds., *Chilies to Chocolate* (Tucson, Ariz., 1992), is a shorter account. Amal Naj, *Peppers* (New York, 1992), is a popular introduction to the subject. For a brilliant study of chilies and other Aztec and Mayan foodstuffs, see Sophie D. Coe, *America's First Cuisines* (Austin, Tex., 1994).

Among the appealing and frequently entertaining books that deal with chili, the dish, are John Thorne, *Serious Pig* (New York, 1996); Jane Stern and Michael Stern, C*hili Nation* (New York, 1998); Martina Neely and William Neely, *Official Chili Cookbook* (New York, 1981); Bill Bridges and Wade Rawson, *The Great American Chili Book* (New York, 1981); Joe E. Cooper, *With or Without Beans* (Dallas, 1952); Frank X. Tolbert, *A Bowl of Red* (New York, 1966); and Linda Stradley, *History and Legends of Chili*, available online at http://whatscookingamerica.net/History/Chili/ChiliHistory.htm.

For a provocative exploration of Mexican food and culture, see Jeffrey M. Pilcher, *¡Que vivian los tamales! Food and the Making of Mexican Identity* (Albuquerque, N.M., 1988). A magnum opus on Mexican cooking is Diana Kennedy, *The Cuisines of Mexico* (New York, 1986).

A fact-filled history of Tex-Mex food is Andrew F. Smith, "Tacos, Enchiladas, and Refried Beans: The Invention of Mexican-American Cookery," research paper for Symposium on Cultural and Historical Aspects of Food, Oregon State University, April 1999, available online at http://food.oregonstate.edu/ref/culture/mexico_smith.html. Additional accounts are offered in Sharon Hudgins, "Red Dust: Powdered Chilis and Chili Powder," in Harlan Walker, ed., *Oxford Symposium 1992: Spicing Up the Palate* (London, 1992), and Keith J. Guenther, "The Development of Mexican-American Cuisine," in Alan Davidson, ed., *Oxford Symposium 1981: National and Regional Styles of Cookery* (London, 1981).

Vivid chronicles of San Antonio include Donald E. Everett, *San Antonio: The Flavor of Its Past, 1845–1898* (San Antonio, Tex., 1975); Frank H. Bushick, *Glamorous Days* (San Antonio, Tex., 1934); and Charles Ramsdell, *San Antonio: A Historical and Pictorial Guide* (Austin, Tex., 1959). A lively piece on chili in San Antonio folklore is Ron Bechtol, "Chili, A San Antonio Tradition," *San Antonio Monthly*, May 1987.

To my knowledge, no one has written a biography of the German-American chili powder innovator, William Gebhardt. Pieces of his story can be gleaned from T. R. Fehrenbach, *The San Antonio Story* (Tulsa, Okla., 1978); *Picturesque San Antonio* (San Antonio, Tex., 1911); and Amy E. Mesch, "William Gebhardt and the Origin of Chili Powder," *Texas Historian*, vol. 53, no. 2 (November 1992). A collection of recipes that use his company's chili powder is assembled in

Mexican Cookery for American Homes (San Antonio, Tex., 1923). The "New York System" chili dogs of Rhode Island are portrayed in *New York Times*, November 13, 2002.

The history of America's other chili incarnations, many concocted by ethnics, is just beginning to be written. Timothy Lloyd, "The Cincinnati Chili Culinary Complex," in Barbara G. Shortridge and James R. Shortridge, eds., *The Taste of American Place: A Reader on Regional and Ethnic Foods* (Lanham, Md., 1998), was the article that awakened me to the ethnic roots of Cincinnati chili. Ron Berler, "Red Hot Guide to Cincinnati Chili," *Cincinnati*, vol. 12, no. 1 (October 1978), adds some interesting nuggets to the dish's history. An interview with Louis Giatras, owner of the Coney Island Famous Wiener Company in Cumberland, Maryland, helped me to record the eatery's story. Timothy Lloyd, "Paterson's Hot Texas Wiener Tradition," *Folklife Center News*, vol. 17, no. 2 (spring 1995), unearths the history of the city's popular fast food.

The American Coney Island website (http://www.americanconeyisland.com/home.htm) provides information on the eatery and its famous product. Two useful articles on the Michigan delight are "Detroit Is Coney Country," *Detroit News*, September 29, 1999, and "Coneycopia," *Detroit Monthly* (June 1996).

An abundance of writing on Caribbean society and culture as well as on the plants, food, and cooking of the region served me well. Several works by Sidney Mintz offer sharp observations: Sidney W. Mintz, *Caribbean Transformations* (Baltimore, 1974); Sidney W. Mintz and Sally Price, eds., *Caribbean Contours* (Baltimore, 1985); and Sidney W. Mintz, *Tasting Food, Tasting Freedom* (Boston, 1996). Raymond Sokolov (1991, mentioned in the introductory section) frequently has suggestive comments on the origins of Latin food. Elizabeth Rozin, *Blue Corn and Chocolate* (New York, 1992), is filled with absorbing details about the culinary culture of the Americas.

Surveys of the tropical plant life of the islands can be quite helpful. Useful material can be gleaned from Wilson Popenoe, *Manual of Tropical and Subtropical Fruits* (New York, 1920); Nigel J. H. Smith, *Tropical Forests and Their Crops* (Ithaca, N.Y., 1992); Gonzalo Fernandez de Oviedo, *Natural History of the West Indies* (Chapel Hill, N.C., 1959); Carl Sauer, *Agricultural Origins and Dispersals* (New York, 1952); and Jonathan Sauer, *Historical Geography of Crop Plants* (Boca Raton, Fla., 1993). A comprehensive discussion of Latin American edible plants is the piece by Carl Sauer, "Cultivated Plants of South and Central America," in Julian H. Steward, ed., *Handbook of South American Indians*, vol. 6 (Washington, D.C., 1950). The same volume contains an essay by Claude Levi-Strauss, "The Use of Wild Plants in Tropical South America." Consult A. Hyatt Verrill, *Foods America Gave the World* (Boston, 1937), for interesting tidbits about food and botany.

Cookbook authors have been churning out handbooks on Caribbean food, although one in English on Dominican cooking is conspicuously lacking. Good overviews of Caribbean food are Linda Wolfe, *The Cooking of the Caribbean Islands* (New York, 1970); Jessica R. Harris, *Sky Juice and Flying Fish* (New York, 1991); and Elisabeth Lambert Ortiz, *The Complete Book of Caribbean Cooking* (New York, 1973). A fact-filled compendium on Caribbean cooking ingredients is Linda Bladholm, *Latin and Caribbean Stores Demystified* (Los Angeles, 2001). Puerto Rican food is introduced in Yvonne Ortiz, *A Taste of Puerto Rico* (New York, 1997); Oswald Rivera, *Puerto Rican Cuisine in America* (New York, 1993); and Dora Romano, *Rice and Beans and Tasty Things* (Floral Park, Puerto Rico, 1998). Maria Josefa Lloria, *A Taste of Old Cuba* (New York, 1994), is one of the better primers on the island's cuisine.

The Puerto Rican experience in New York is analyzed in Nicholas Lemann, "The Other Underclass," *Atlantic* (December 1991). I leaned on a variety of materials for an understanding of East Harlem and La Marqueta. Among them were the guidebooks by Vilma Liacourias Chantiles (1984), Irene Sax (1984), Kate Simon (1971), and Zelda Stern (1980) referred to in the introductory section. An issue of *Nosh News*, a lively newsletter on New York City foodways, tells a brief story of the market and the Puerto Rican neighborhood: *Nosh News*, no. 7 (Fall/Winter, 2000).

The Dominicans, the fastest-growing immigrant group in New York City, are now getting their due. A nice introduction is Silvia-Torres Saillant and Ramona Hernandez, *The Dominican Americans* (Westport, Conn., 1988). Patricia Pessar, *A Visa for a Dream* (Boston, 1995), highlights the Latin immigrants. Luis Guarnizo is one of the leading social scientists to investigate this group, particularly its entrepreneurial development: Luis Guarnizo, "One Country in Two: Dominican-Owned Firms in New York and in the Dominican Republic," Ph.D. dissertation, Johns Hopkins University, 1993; Guarnizo, "Los Dominican Yorks: The Making of a Binational Society," *Annals of the American Academy of Political and Social Science*, no. 533 (1994). Peggy Levitt illuminates the island's immigrants in "A Todos Les Llamo Primo (I Call Everyone Cousin): The Social Basis for Latino Small Business," in Marilyn Halter, ed., *New Migrants in the Marketplace* (Amherst, Mass., 1995), and in *Transnational Villagers* (Berkeley, 2001).

The story of Goya was pieced together from interviews, company publications and press releases, and newspaper and magazine articles. The Goya Foods Collection at the Smithsonian National Museum of American History's Archive Center has gathered many of the pertinent writings on the history of the company. It is weak, however, on internal correspondence and memoranda that might reveal Goya's marketing strategy.

Many conversations and several interviews with Cresencia Torres, owner of the Manna restaurant, revealed Goya's critical role in the life of a small food business.

Interviews with Goya executive Conrad Colon were invaluable for helping me to chart the development of the business. Public relations director Rafael Toro filled in some important gaps. Former Goya media consultant Karen Sperling provided a variety of helpful leads and suggestions.

Among the numerous articles covering the New Jersey–based business are "Goya: A Lot More Than Black Beans and Sofrito," *Business Week,* December 7, 1987; "Run to the Supermarket and Pick Me Up Some Cactus," *Business Week,* June 20, 1994; "A Taste of Home: Goya Foods Seems to Speak to All Hispanics," *Dallas Morning News,* February 19, 1997; "Much More Than Meat and Potatoes," *News Parade,* November 13, 1994; "Goya: Spanish Flavor in U.S.," *New York Times,* April 23, 1979; "Crossover Dreams: Goya Wants Non-Hispanics to Taste Its Line," *Broward Daily Business Review,* March 21, 1997; Leo Martin Lopez, "Hey, Big Vendor," *Latino Leaders,* vol. 2, no. 4 (August–September 2001).

The bodega and the Dominican-owned supermarket have been frequently profiled in the press. Informative articles include "To Hispanics in U.S., a Bodega, or Grocery, Is a Vital Part of Life," *Wall Street Journal,* March 15, 1985; "Between Two Worlds: Dominicans in New York," *New York Times,* September 16, 1991; "Thriving Where Others Won't Go," *New York Times,* January 7, 1992; and "Bodegas Find Prosperity Amid Change," *New York Times,* November 19, 1986. Interviews with Luis Salcedo, director of the National Supermarket Association, provided valuable knowledge on the Dominican food business.

New Jersey's Cuban émigré community is discussed in Barbara Cunningham, ed., *The New Jersey Ethnic Experience* (Union City, N.J., 1977). Colorful pictures of the ethnics are sketched in "Moors and Christians in Union City, N.J.," *Washington Post,* December 21, 1988, and "Along 90 Blocks of New Jersey, a New World of Latin Tastes," *New York Times,* December 11, 1991.

Quotation sources for Chapter 7:
Page
   135   "Martha has raven hair": Bushick 1934, p. 99.
135–136 "A Mexican bootblack": Ibid., p. 98.
   136   "Mustangs, mules, donkeys": Everett 1975, p. 5.
   136   "travelers, rancheros": Ibid., p. 6.
   136   "delectable meats": Ramsdell 1959, p. 274.
   136   "sauntering Mexicans": Everett 1975, p. 5.

136   "fat, swarthy Mexican mater-familias": Ramsdell 1959, p. 273.

137   "kind of hash": Ibid., p. 272.

138   "with the aid of meat": Andrews 1995, p. 2.

138   "mild red chiles": Coe 1994, p. 93.

139   "red chile and tomatoes": Ibid., p. 115.

139–140 "flowers groweth along the stalks": Tolbert 1966, p. 30.

140   "very hote, fuming": Andrews 1995, p. 26.

141   "tonic upon the system": Tolbert 1966, p. 69.

141   "real Mexican tang": *Picturesque San Antonio* 1911, p. 27.

141   "delightful seasoning": Hudgins 1992, p. 112.

141   "capture the glamour": Mesch 1992, p. 13.

142   "diaper pin": Cooper 1952, p. 102.

143   "roast beef, roast pork": Berler 1978, p. 62.

146   "it was so American": *Detroit News*, September 29, 1999.

146   "there's one on every corner": Ibid.

148   "beautiful cool leaves": Oviedo 1959, p. 80.

150–151 "roar mambos": Simon 1971, p. 86.

152   "we sold only to bodegas": *New York Times*, April 23, 1979.

152   "history of most of our customers": Halter 1995, p. 131.

152–153 "something small and quick": *New York Times*, November 19, 1986.

153   "talk daily to bodega": *Crain's News*, November 23–29, 1992.

154   "They are very industrious": *New York Times*, January 7, 1992.

156   "we print the labels": *Dallas Morning News*, February 19, 1997.

157   "the scent of peppercorns": Rivera 1993, p. 107.

159   "older Hispanics": *Orlando Sentinel*, October 24, 1996.

159   "typical Cuban things": *Dallas Morning News*, February 17, 1997.

160   "follow the trend of immigrating Hispanics": *Business Week*, June 20, 1994.

160   "selling the same product": *Hispanic Business Monthly*, January–February 1982.

160   "Immigrants have real loyalty": *Wall Street Journal*, April 15, 1998.

162   "strange vegetarian food": *News Parade*, November 13, 1994.

162   "the way Italian food is now": *Newsweek*, May 17, 1982.

162   "segregated from the normal foods": *Sunday Star-Ledger*, October 4, 1981.

INDEX